WHAT PEOPLE ARE SAYING ABOUT
THE SIMPLE GOSPEL

'Ben is a leading gospel communicator who has a razor-sharp ability to connect the good news of Jesus Christ to people from all backgrounds, ages and stages. I've seen him turn the most difficult questions into gospel opportunities with an ease I've rarely encountered. This book will sharpen your focus and enhance your ability to communicate the gospel – and for that reason, you should buy it and absorb the contents.' – **Carl Beech, CVM**

'Ben Jack has done us a huge favour. Confusion about the gospel is rife. Gospel dilution is widespread. Ben calls us back to the beauty, power and centrality of the gospel. As a gifted evangelist he also addresses the issues that make us tongue-tied and weak at the knees when it comes to making much of Jesus. This book is a great gift to the body of Christ to remind and call us back to "that which is of first importance". Read it, mark it, inwardly digest it. Buy a box and give away a bunch to your friends, co-labourers, evangelists, pastors, youth workers, and aspiring preachers.' – **Dr. Bill Hogg, North American Missiologist, C2C Network**

'I absolutely loved reading this informative and inspiring look at the gospel, which is still the power of God unto salvation. *The Simple Gospel* is a must-read to help you understand the impact of the gospel and be sharpened as you share it.' – **Rev. Mark Greenwood, National Evangelist and Head of Evangelism, Elim Churches**

'With real-life stories, experiences and strong Christology, Ben unpacks the very kernel of the Christian faith and challenges each of us to neither add nor detract from it but to advance it with full confidence. This book is both timely and relevant in a world that screams at us to compromise the truth of this transforming good news for popularity, and it's an important reminder to all evangelicals of what makes us evangelicals in the first place. Thank you, Ben, for taking us beyond four points and allowing us to celebrate a fully-orbed gospel of the kingdom. This is a book packed with wisdom, courage and truth, engaging from start to finish and aimed to ground its readers afresh in the good news.' – **Mitch, Evangelist, Crown Jesus Ministries**

'Ben is a walking, talking, theological encyclo-paedia! His focused heart for the lost, coupled with a deep knowledge of who we are and whose we are, is clear in this book. If you want to get your head around what the gospel is and why we've got to get serious about sharing it with anyone and everyone, this is the perfect place to start. I'll be sharing this with my whole team and recommend that you do too.' – **Lindz West, Evangelist, Light/LZ7**

THE SIMPLE GOSPEL

the
SIMPLE
GOSPEL

Understanding and
sharing the Jesus story

BEN JACK

First published in Great Britain in 2018 by The Message Trust
Lancaster House, Harper Road
Manchester, M22 4RG, UK

ISBN 978-1-9999036-4-0
eISBN 978-1-9999036-5-7

Author photograph: Rachael Silvester
Cover design and typesetting: Simon Baker for Message Creative

CONTENTS

INTRODUCTION

'The call to enter the kingdom is not merely a welcome to all its privileges, but is also a summons to serve all its interests, and its most vital interest is the proclamation to all the world of Jesus as saviour and Lord. Evangelism, accordingly, is the business of every Christian.' – T.B Kilpatrick[1]

He looked at me with a wry and somewhat sinister smile as he considered the words I had just shared with him. Finally, after what seemed like an eternity, he responded, his thick Italian accent injecting every word with a surprisingly sharp venom:

'It is not good that you have met me. You are lucky we are not in Italy where I have my pistol.'

He turned his back on me and walked away. And there, late one summer evening, on a street in the middle of Brooklyn, ended my first evangelistic conversation with a Neo-fascist.[2] Thankfully, not all my attempts at evangelism have ended this way, but it was a powerful reminder that it's not always plain sailing.

Perhaps this isn't the best way to begin this short book about getting back to the basics of sharing the gospel. Sure, it makes the point that evangelistic dialogue doesn't always go to plan (unless your goal is to be threatened with a pistol) but for many reading this, we have already jumped a few steps ahead of where you are right now. Being threatened with physical harm in response to sharing the gospel assumes a level of evangelistic dialogue that you may never have stepped into.

Now, before you go running for the hills, let me be clear: this is a book of encouragement, not critique or rebuke. This is not another 'down on the church' polemic. However, before we can begin to encourage and affirm the positive way forward, we must acknowledge and address the gospel-shaped elephant (or lack thereof) in the room. We have a big problem in the church today: put simply, we have stopped preaching the gospel. Heck, forget preaching for a moment; many in the church have stopped faithfully *sharing* the gospel in any capacity, within their day to day interactions.

There are all sorts of reasons why we might find ourselves avoiding or sidelining evangelism. Some lack confidence in their ability to communicate God's message. Some are so gripped by the fear of man that they worry more about what people might think than about what God has called us to. Some think evangelism is the job of 'professional Christians'. Some don't even see the need to share the gospel with the world. Oh, and then there's Netflix.

Let me assure you from the outset: I get it. I'm not trying to be flippant, but the reality is that many people find it so hard to share their faith that they simply never do it. Even though evangelism could be considered my full-time 'job', I still find it hugely challenging at times. Funnily enough, I am actually far more comfortable preaching the gospel from a stage to a large crowd than engaging in interpersonal conversation with strangers. The fact is that these one-on-one interactions carry a much greater risk of personal rejection, which is surely something none of us actively enjoys or embraces.

The question is: even when evangelism is hard, even when it hurts, even when it costs us, do we know what the gospel is and are we willing to have a go at sharing it with a world in need?

The gospel is the only hope the world has to know its true identity and to be given assurance of an eternal heaven, rather than eternal hell. Some will wince at that statement, believing the idea of hell to be antiquated and out of step with a contemporary understanding of the 'nice' Jesus of the New Testament. Even if you believe there is a hell, the idea of acknowledging it to those who are heading for it may make you intensely uncomfortable. So many who come to faith today are fed a diet of 'God loves you' rhetoric that is divorced from a meaningful under-standing of just what makes God's love so amazing. Stay with me, because we will unpack the importance of the reality of heaven and hell in due course.

The implication of the gospel being a matter of eternal life and death should sober and stir us to the importance of sharing the good news with a perishing world, for we have the antidote to the fatal disease of sin. There is a hell, but none need go there, and when we understand that, we understand what it truly means to say and live out the words 'God loves you' with authenticity, integrity and power.

Proclaiming the gospel is not merely an item on a checklist for Christians, it is a fundamental part of who we are as new creations of the gospel. Failure to share the good news is a failure to live in the full identity that God has made possible for us through Jesus Christ. The commissioning words of Christ to his followers at the climax of Matthew's gospel are both an authorisation and a promise of the life that follows submission to his Lordship (Mt. 28:16-20). You will not be able to stop sharing his good news once you have received it.

To be sure, our salvation does not hinge on how many people we witness to; we are saved by faith alone, not by faith *and* works.[3] However, if we claim to be in relationship with Jesus Christ but show no desire

4

to share his hope with the world, this should pose challenging questions about the authenticity of the faith we profess. It is not my intention to cause you to question your salvation in these pages, but it should be the intention of us all to work out our salvation with the greatest respect to God: to who he is, what he has done, and what that means for our life, both now and in the perfection of heaven that awaits all who trust in the Lord (Phil. 2:12; Rom. 10:9). I believe this book will help you to do just that by exploring what it truly means to move from rebellion to rescue, from problem to solution, from chaos to peacemaker.

Having been saved from the consequences of our rebellion against God by the death and resurrection of Jesus, we are called and equipped by him to take this very same gospel into the world, that all who have ears to hear can also be saved. We become co-labourers with God (1 Cor. 3:9), ambassadors of the kingdom, ministers of reconciliation (2 Cor. 5:18-20), Spirit-empowered witnesses into all the world (Acts 1:8).

The Simple Gospel

Chapter One explores the idea of the simple gospel, and addresses the question of why so many Christians are failing to meaningfully share the gospel in more detail. Chapters Two and Three examine the preaching of Jesus, Peter and Paul, and ask what we can learn about the gospel from the way it is proclaimed through the New Testament. Chapter Four explores what we can learn about the concerns and interests of the world from the culture around us (particularly pop culture), and how we might use cultural connections to help the world better understand the gospel message. Chapters Five and Six bring us home with an explanation of the identity of Jesus at the heart of the gospel, an exploration of our gospel identity in light of who he is, and a look at what that means for sharing the gospel with the world. Along the way, we will consider a few weighty theological ideas, including the kingdom of God, the identity of Jesus, the Trinity, the saving work of the cross and the resurrection, heaven, hell, and more, as we attempt to ground ourselves in the truth of the gospel.

That being said, this is not a one-stop guide to gospel doctrine, and nor does it offer a step-by-step roadmap for personal witness. There are plenty of excellent books that accomplish these tasks admirably, and some recommendations can be found in the Endnotes and Further Reading sections. Rather, this book is intended as a conversation starter, a call to rethink the outworking of our faith and, by focusing on the gospel itself, to get serious about proclaiming the good news to a world that is perishing (1 Cor.

1:18). We will address the six most common reasons for not sharing the gospel (outlined in Chapter One) as we reconfirm what the gospel really is and why followers of Christ must share it, not out of religious duty but from transformed hearts that desire, as God does, for none to perish (2 Pet. 3:9). My hope is that, after finishing this book, you will begin or continue to faithfully share the gospel with others, while pursuing a deeper understanding of the gospel through ongoing study of the Bible and other resources that will help you on your journey.

I have included a basic outline of the theology of the gospel, the core tenets of the good news, for your reference, and you will also find discussion questions for each chapter alongside the Endnotes. Annotations are collected at the back so as not to distract from the text, but I would encourage you to take a look for one or two asides that will either make you laugh, roll your eyes, or offer some deeper thoughts and insights that I am confident you will find beneficial.

With all that in mind, let's dive into the simple gospel and discover our equally simple yet eternally significant role as its messengers.

CHAPTER ONE

THE SIMPLE GOSPEL

I recently attempted to decorate my living room, an endeavour that ultimately had me asking myself, 'Why did I bother starting this?' DIY is not my strong suit, and a job that would probably have taken the average person just a few hours dragged on for several days. It turns out that all those years of playing video games didn't prepare me for adult life at all.[4]

The main problem was that I overcomplicated the process by not having the necessary tools at my disposal to get the job done as efficiently as possible. I ended up creating an almighty mess that took even longer to clean up and, worst of all, the end result is not as well presented as it might have been. I tried to muddle through and get the job done quickly, whereas good preparation would have equipped me for a far simpler, smoother and more successful experience.

If only overcomplication was limited to the misery of decorating your house (I appreciate that some readers will enjoy decorating, but we're going to have to agree to disagree on that one). Truth be told, life is complicated, and humanity has a habit of making it even more so. Gandhi famously said, 'Live simply so that others may simply live,' yet despite our best efforts to simplify and improve the world through technological advances, the sharing of ideas and the championing of basic human rights, Gandhi's words seem more relevant today than ever before. Indeed, the world seems to get *more* complex rather than less so as time goes by, and we see a greater disparity between those who have and those who have not.

I think Gandhi actually stumbled upon something profound about the sharing of the gospel, without realising it. If we were to reword his statement as follows, perhaps it would strike a chord for those of us who are concerned with the proclamation of the good news:

'Preach simply so that others may simply live.'

The two explanations of the gospel that I hear most often can be summarised fairly simply:

1. You have done bad things, you are a sinner and are heading for hell, but in his love and grace God has provided Jesus, who died and rose again, and through faith in him you can be saved and enter heaven.

2. Is your life hard? Have you experienced heartbreak and suffering? Do you have low self-esteem? Well, God loves you. Put your trust in him and you will come to know your true identity. He will help you in this life and you can know true happiness.

Perhaps you have shared the gospel in one of these two ways, or in a variation on them. I know I have in the past. It is worth taking a moment to reflect on these basic explanations of the gospel to consider what is good and helpful, and what is lacking.

Neither of these explanations in fact represents the full truth of the good news. They both contain truth about the gospel, but neither is sufficient in expressing who Jesus is, what he has done, and what that means for humanity. Even the oft-cited scripture from John 3:16, undoubtedly the most famous of all Bible verses and celebrated by Martin Luther as 'the heart of the Bible, the gospel in miniature,' is not a sufficient explanation of the gospel in isolation.[5] God does indeed love the world so much that he has provided his only Son to save us from death and give us eternal life, but this is not the complete message of the gospel, and nor is it the good news that Jesus himself announced when he arrived on the preaching scene two thousand years ago, with the words, 'Repent, for the kingdom of heaven is at hand' (Mark 1:14-15). I agree with Luther that John 3:16 is the gospel in miniature, and therefore a great place to start, but more is needed. We should desire to know and articulate the gospel as fully as we can.[6]

'Preaching simply' does not mean preaching a watered-down, more palatable message. Paul warns that this will lead to the preaching of no gospel at all (Gal. 1:6-9). 'Preaching simply' means being able to explain the full gospel in all its power and authority, clearly, to any audience who would have ears to hear.

Good Advice?

Gandhi offered profound advice and wisdom in a quest to better the world, but we must not fall into the trap of offering the gospel merely as good advice in the hope of bringing positive social change.[7] The gospel is not good advice, it is the announcement of the good news of the coming kingdom; the invitation to turn from rebellion against the King of the universe and choose submission to his Lordship; the gateway to life in all its fullness, the life for which humanity was created. Good advice can be heeded or ignored, perhaps with little consequence. While the gospel invitation can also be taken up or forgotten, the consequences are both temporally *and* eternally significant.

To preach the gospel is to offer a simple invitation – do you want to live?

And this is a deeply important question, for if the answer is 'yes' the gospel declares that there is only one true life: life *in* the kingdom of God. On the off-chance that the answer is 'no' (and with suicide rates in the developed world being so high, this is a tragic possibility), the gospel declares that there is hope for you too. The life you may not want to live is not the life you were created for anyway. Your dissatisfaction at the life you live is shared by the God who created you for more, and who has provided the way by which you can know true life, fulfilled life.

One of my great heroes, C.S. Lewis, came to faith in Christ partly because Christianity helped him to reconcile a rational understanding of the universe with a satisfying explanation of why we experience longing and desire in this life. That very idea speaks into the heart of the gospel: not simply that we are sinners who need a saviour to get us to heaven, but that we were created to dwell in the perfect kingdom of our heavenly Father God, a kingdom that can actually be experienced in this life, before being perfected in what we would call heaven. The reason we experience longing and desire is because we were created for a kingdom that is not yet fully present, but that has been initiated in the work of Christ and will be perfected when he returns. But how many of us actually present the gospel in these terms? Then again, how many of us even want to?

The Bad News

If the good news of Jesus Christ is the hope for the world, and if we have already received it ourselves, why have so many lost the drive, desire, or confidence to share it? There are likely more reasons than we have time to explore here, but six stand out as especially problematic.

1. THE ME-CENTRED PROBLEM

When the gospel is presented as more-or-less exclusively the answer to my existential crisis – 'Who am I?' – then the application of the gospel to my life is in danger of becoming more-or-less exclusively self-centred. This is not helped by overly consumerist approaches to church that promote personal satisfaction as key to the worship experience, rather than personal sacrifice as key to the worshipful life. It is easy to point the finger disapprovingly at the younger generations for the narcissism that seems to run rife within their ranks, but the truth is that the preaching of an almost exclusively existential gospel (whilst not wrong in its assertion of the gospel as the key to your true identity) has contributed to narcissism, self-centredness and self-righteousness being all too present among the people of God. For the person who thinks the gospel is all about them, there is little incentive to inconvenience themselves for the benefit of others.[8]

2. THE HYPER-GRACE PROBLEM

God is so gracious that people don't really need to seek his forgiveness; surely his grace will cover all. This idea leads us down the road of two hugely problematic beliefs. The first, antinomianism, is the idea that we can essentially abuse God's grace with no consequence. God will forgive us, whatever happens, so continuing to sin is not really a problem. Taken to its fullest outworking, antinomianism doesn't actively *seek* forgiveness for sin, it merely asserts that all sin will be forgiven by virtue of God's grace.

This leads to the next big problem: universalism. This is the idea that, on judgement day, God will save everyone and none will perish. As much as I would love to believe that none will spend an eternity separated from God, neither of these beliefs reflects what the Bible actually teaches (we will explore this further in Chapter Six); ultimately, they make a mockery of the gospel and the actions of Christ upon the cross. In antinomian and universalist thinking, there can be little incentive to share the gospel for the salvation of souls, as sin needs no true repentance and all will spend eternity with God, whatever happens in this life.

3. THE BORN-WRONG PROBLEM

John Wimber lamented that preaching a faulty gospel produces faulty Christians.[9] The born-wrong problem occurs when listeners hear a weak presentation of the gospel and so are 'born wrong' into their new Christian faith. The outworking of this for evangelism can be the adoption of false ideas, such as antinomianism and universalism, or that some Christians simply do not know that personal witness and evangelism are part of the Christian life. These believers are particularly likely to view evangelism as the job of the professional (the pastor, the missionary), rather than a responsibility and calling upon all believers.

4. THE FEAR OF MAN PROBLEM

There are many Christians who have a strong desire to share their faith but are paralysed by fear. As the western world, in particular, becomes increasingly pluralistic and obsessed with 'political correctness', the Christian claim of the exclusivity of Jesus as the way, the truth and the life seems less and less publicly acceptable.[10] I'm sure we can all empathise with this problem on some level. As a Christian of twenty-five years, with more than fifteen years' experience as an evangelist, I can assure you that I have my fair share of stories where I 'bottled it' because of the fear of man, and yet the Bible calls us to be bold, trusting in the Lord to help us, whatever persecution may come. We are to be an unashamed people, confident in the saving power of God (Rom. 1:16).

5. THE FIT-FOR-PURPOSE PROBLEM

Related to the fear of man problem is the question, 'How could God use little ol' me, with all my weaknesses, flaws and failings?' There is much to be said about what qualifies a person for kingdom service, but for focus in this book we will reflect mainly on knowing the truth of the gospel deeply, so that we are able to live it well and explain it simply at any given opportunity. Wonderfully, God is in the business of taking people who think they can't, and turning them into people who do; taking our weakness, and making his power perfect through it (2 Cor. 12:9).

6. THE HOW PROBLEM

Finally, there are those who have a desire to share but don't know how to explain the gospel to those they talk to. The knowledge of what the gospel is and an ability to explain it clearly to others is lacking, and so they do not have the confidence to enter into Jesus-centred conversations. In many respects this is the easiest of the problems to fix, requiring only a better understanding of the Jesus story and perhaps a few basic conversational techniques.

Whatever our reasons for failing to share the good news, God desires to equip and empower us – you! – to be his messengers in this world and to share in the joy of the rescue mission he has initiated. He does not use you begrudgingly, but delights in partnering with you to see the hope you have received, lived and proclaimed for all to see and hear. The best way to discover (or rediscover) a passion for evangelism is to return to the wonder of the gospel itself.

Understanding The Gospel

'If you can't explain it simply, you don't understand it well enough.'

This quote is often accredited to Albert Einstein, and variations of it have been linked with other great thinkers and intellects over the years.[11] Fortunately, we don't need to have Einstein levels of genius to understand the gospel. The good news is not merely an academic subject to be studied, but a past, present and future reality to be received. However, we should put in the effort to understand the gospel as deeply as we possibly can, for a deep understanding of the gospel will help us to take what we have received and share it simply with the world.

This depth of study and reflection is not just an exercise in theological navel-gazing, but an attempt to understand what the good news truly is, how it impacts our lives, and how we can share the message with the world. A primary way to figure this out is to look at what the first preachers of the gospel understood the good news to be, and how it shaped their lives and witness. In the next couple of chapters we will do just that, but at this point it is worth posing an important question: How much time do you spend simply thinking and praying about the significance of the ministry of Jesus that led him to the cross? Considering afresh just what it was that caused God to send his one and only Son to die for us, and why Jesus allowed himself to hang in that place of suffering and experience that awful death? Meditating upon what it really means that Christ is risen, ascended and will one day return?

'Context is king' is a mantra that I often repeat when teaching on how to study the Bible. In Chapter

Four we will think about the context (culture) *into* which we take the gospel, and how to make the most of the culture around us for gospel opportunity. However, to truly understand the gospel we must be prepared to intentionally engage with God's holy word, *understanding* it in its biblical context before we can *apply* it in our present context. To understand the Bible then, alongside submission to the Spirit's power for the task, we must engage with two basic questions:

WHAT DID THE ORIGINAL AUTHOR INTEND TO SAY TO HIS AUDIENCE?

As shocking as it may seem, the biblical writers didn't specifically have you in mind when they were crafting their work; they wrote for a specific audience. Understanding what the author was saying to his intended audience is essential if we are to make sense of the Bible.

WHAT DOES THAT MEAN FOR US TODAY?

God had us all in mind when the Bible was written. His holy word is still the primary way by which he speaks today, and our means for understanding who he is. If the Bible is just a collection of old stories and theological ideas that were only relevant to the original intended audience, all is lost. Jesus died for human beings, not just theologians, and it is in the application of God's Word today that we truly become his followers.[12]

We can't grapple with the second question until we've come to some understanding of the first, so no skipping ahead! To start with, we're going to need some context, as we can never hope to understand what the original author intended to say without at least a little understanding of the context in which (and to which) the passage was written.[13]

And here's why I'm such a stickler for context (and why you should be, too) because, taken out of context, we can pretty much make the Bible say whatever we want and use it to justify any belief. After all, the Bible says at one point that there is no God![14] At best, this is a naive and misguided approach to God's Word that will lead to an incorrect understanding of what it teaches and its application to our lives. At worst, the Bible becomes deliberately subverted and used to justify horrendous acts in the name of God.[15] Many of the objections I face in my evangelism are over things the Bible teaches. Some of these are just misunderstandings and can be corrected. Others are indeed true biblical teaching, but I can only help others to understand the context of that teaching – its validity, relevance and application today – if I have taken the time to consider these things myself.

A deeper understanding of the truth, discovered through a commitment to exploring the context in which and to which it was written, will help us to become more effective messengers. Likewise, an awareness of the context (culture) for our evangelism is important if we are to understand how best to deliver the message of the gospel to any given audience. Ultimately, the task of reading and understanding the Bible, and the task of bringing the message of the gospel to any culture, hinges on one crucial thing above all else – submission to and reliance upon the Spirit of God to enlighten and empower. As the theologian Haddon Robinson said:

> Ultimately God is more interested in developing messengers than messages, and because the Holy Spirit confronts us primarily through the Bible, we must learn to listen to God before speaking for God.[16]

Reflection and study of the Word are essential as we try to understand the gospel more deeply, both for the purposes of proclamation and, importantly, to move us once more to a place of awe and worship of who God is and what he has done. The gospel has lost none of its power to save. The same gospel Peter preached at Pentecost is still bringing people to life today. To find success in both the visible and verbal aspects of our evangelism we must take the time, as the apostles did, to know Jesus *and* the good news that declares his glory.[17] So let us do exactly that now, as we explore the gospel as proclaimed by Jesus.

CHAPTER TWO

THE KINGDOM GOSPEL

I've always had a bit of a rebellious side. If I was cool enough to pull off the biker jacket and toothpick look I would have been that guy (I'm not, and I'm pretty sure that in the history of the world only James Dean and Steve McQueen could get away with it), nonchalantly standing around, doing my own thing, cold-eyeing any and all authority figures that came by and daring them to tell me to 'move along'.

I remember, as a teenager, getting into an extended power struggle with my chemistry teacher over the course of one school term. For some reason, I assumed she was out to get me, so I did everything I could to undermine her authority as teacher, to belittle her and build myself up in front of my classmates. This involved everything from your basic teenage sassing, through to an unfortunate incident with a VHS tape that I decided to hide from her during one lesson (in the goggles box for safety, which I thought was quite witty), only to then return it to the video player after she left the room to call the tech guy for help. Cue one red-faced teacher when he walks in and simply presses play.

Why she left the room a second time I will never know. At the time, I just thought it was the universe confirming that I was the hero of this particular story, and affording me another opportunity to get one over on her. I took the tape out again and, much to her frustration when she returned, once again the video didn't play. Take that, authority![18]

I got caught of course, and my lunchtime social activities took an unpleasant hit for quite some time after that. In reality, the problem was not my teacher, but me. My insecurity that she didn't like me drove me to reject any help, wisdom or knowledge that she tried to share with me as part of my studies. I thought she was unworthy of my respect, and so I rejected her as a suitable teacher and authority figure.

Sometimes it is appropriate to reject or challenge an authority figure or system. The elected leader who has failed to make good on their promises or lead with integrity, for example; the legal system that exists to protect all equally, yet favours the strong and the rich; the dictator who forces their way to power by exploiting their own people for personal gain.

Interestingly, we have moved away from a society that sees the anti-authority rebel as the cool and mysterious outsider to a culture in which 'authority scepticism' is more or less the standard position. We've become wary of the concept of authority due to its abuses. History is littered with tales of kings and queens who have abused their power and their people, and so we – in the west – can now surely breathe a sigh of relief that we live in enlightened, democratic times, free from the tyrannous authority of old, to which the average person had no choice but to submit. Yet, ultimately, this is misguided thinking. Whilst we have created a democratic system in which the average person can have a say in choosing their own leaders, we have not yet solved the problem of authority abuse and power corruption. It's almost as if human beings aren't perfect....

Anti-authoritarianism potentially poses a big problem for faithful gospel preaching today. The central message of the gospel hinges on an important truth: you are not the centre of the universe, you were created *by* the King *for* the King. Explanations of rebellion against God (sin), the saving work of Christ and the perfection of God's eternal kingdom all converge around this truth and only make sense when set within this proper context of the gospel.

I know what you're thinking: This evangelism thing is already challenging enough, Ben. Are you suggesting we make it harder by deliberately presenting it in a way that will inevitably be met with scepticism or disdain by western culture?

Okay, so preaching the gospel of the kingdom to contemporary western audiences can sometimes feel like attempting the already Herculean task of swimming the English Channel, but with added lead weights hanging from all four of your limbs, while a huge yacht of partygoers glides alongside you, taunting you every stroke of the way (in between mouthfuls of tasty-looking canapés). But, irrespective of whether we think it will make our task more challenging, we must be primarily concerned with the *content* of our message. We must not settle for palatable but empty versions of the gospel that do not match up with Jesus' own understanding of the good news.

The Good News According To Jesus

Mark's gospel records Jesus leading the preaching charge at the outset of his ministry, with a simple message:

> 'The time has come,' he said. 'The kingdom of God has come near. Repent and believe the good news!' (Mk 1:15, NIV)

This is the simplest summary we have of Jesus' essential message: the message of the coming kingdom.[19] In other words, 'Change direction! You're going the wrong way, running away from the perfect kingdom of God. The world is about to be forever changed by my life, ministry, death and resurrection – the King is here to make things right'.[20]

By his 'essential message', I mean that whether addressing the crowds in the Sermon on the Mount, dealing with the Pharisees, engaging in one-to-one encounters with those who sought him out, telling parables, or intimately conversing with his disciples, Jesus remained consistent in his kingdom focus:

> Jesus is shown so consistently proclaiming the kingdom that it was undeniably central to his message.[21]

Clearly, the announcement of the coming kingdom was core to Jesus' message, but how much importance does that hold for us today? After all, the message the disciples proclaimed was much less focused on the kingdom, and more on Jesus himself (more on that in Chapter Three). Some would argue that the kingdom language Jesus used was deliberately chosen to speak to his Jewish audience in both familiar and subversive ways, and therefore is not immediately relevant to contemporary gospel sharing.[22]

This book is concerned with helping us get back to a simple expression of the gospel so that we can effectively share it in any context – back to basics. For Jesus, 'basics' meant helping his audience understand something of God's kingdom, its imminence and significance. To strip the announcement of the King and his kingdom from the story of the gospel is like trying to explain the plot of Harry Potter without mention of wizards and magic – it loses both context and substance, without which the story becomes a shadow of its true self. In literature, this is problematic, but when explaining the truth of life itself (and the consequences of rejecting God's rule) context and substance are not just tools for *understanding* the truth, they *are* the very truth we are sharing. Our message will be deeply – possibly fatally – compromised if we fail to engage with the core truth upon which it hinges.

The message of the kingdom is not merely an aspect of the good news, it is the way by which we make sense of *everything* about the good news![23] Keeping the kingdom truth at the centre of the good news is not only important to the integrity of the gospel message, it is essential if we are to help people to understand why the gospel is not simply a nice idea, but the truth that will bring freedom to all who accept it as such.

Reclaiming Authority

Rejection of authority is nothing new, of course. Perhaps the most famous of all the parables, and certainly the most frequently used in gospel preaching (including my own), is that of the prodigal son (Lk. 15:11-32). Jesus tells the story of a young man who is no longer satisfied with living under the authority of his father. Graciously (but no doubt heartbroken) his father grants the request for early inheritance and the young man strikes out on his own, authority-free path. It is the grace and love of the father that allows the man to return when he inevitably hits rock bottom, not as a slave but as a son.

This is a wonderful parable from which to preach the gospel, but it only fully makes sense when understood in kingdom terms. We, as the rebellious (sinful) creations of God, do not return to the household of the Father to continue in the rebellious behaviour that left us in the pigsty!

We return from our rebellion in the hope that we will not be rejected, only to find that our reception is warmer than we could have hoped for: we are accepted on better terms than we dared believe possible, and given the right to be called children of God (Jn 1:12). But God remains the head of the household – more fully, the King – and we submit to his rule and reign over our lives so that we do not return to the pigsty from which we have been saved. This submission brings freedom, restoration, assurance of salvation, intimacy and peace with the Father – the King. It is the life we were created for; fulfilment and salvation are found nowhere else.[24]

In an anti-authoritarian culture, preaching the authority of the King need not be a painful exercise. In fact, I wonder if we have an amazing opportunity today to contrast the perfection of Christ's rule and reign against society's frustration at the imperfect rule and reign of our leaders, and even our inability to successfully lead our own lives much of the time. Rejection of God's authority often comes down to the idolatrous belief that we know better, that we are the best leaders of our own lives. I've even heard it put in these terms: 'God doesn't deserve my respect. What has he ever done for me?' Suddenly, we find ourselves in the chemistry classroom again, rebelling against our perception of someone, rather than the truth of who they are and how they feel about us.

Here, then, are five aspects of God's rule and reign that could be highly impactful when attempting to share the gospel today. These will help people to understand why he alone is worthy of Lordship in their lives and over this universe:

1. OUR KING IS POWERFUL (GOD IS LOGICAL)

God is the creator of the universe, and therefore the only one *worthy* of ultimate authority over creation. God, as first cause, is more logical and plausible than the 'something from nothing' alternative proposed by scientific naturalism. (Gen. 1:1)

2. OUR KING IS GOOD (GOD IS MORALLY SATISFYING)

God does not abuse his power or his people. However frustrated you are about injustice, God is infinitely more so! Unlike earthly leaders, God's character can be trusted; he always keeps his promises. Conversation around morality, ethics, injustice and righteousness speaks to the reality of our good King. (Ps. 100)

3. OUR KING IS A SERVANT (GOD HAS REVEALED HIMSELF)

Jesus lays aside his crown of glory in heaven to step into our world and serve the very humanity that has rejected him, that they may turn from rebellion to life. He is the Servant King, the most significant and influential figure in all of human history. Posing the question, 'Who is Jesus Christ?' is a compelling conversation starter. (Mt. 20:25-28)

4. OUR KING IS GRACIOUS (GOD TRANSFORMS LIVES)

God will not force his kingship upon you, he will allow you to chose it for yourself. But, like all choices, a rejection of his kingdom brings consequences. Look at the world – from war to suicide, self-harm to extreme poverty – we live in troubling times. But this is the world we should expect if the Bible is true about the consequences of rebellion against God, about making ourselves kings instead of submitting to God's rightful reign. The King offers hope to his people, even in their rebellion: a life can be transformed – this world can be transformed – because of what Jesus has done. (1 Jn. 4:7-19)

5. OUR KING IS RETURNING (GOD IS THE ANSWER)

God's rule will one day be perfectly realised in his eternal kingdom. Whatever fears you may have about the immediate future, or about what lies beyond this life, the perfection of God's kingdom offers hope for living right today, and assurance of what is to come after death. The tragic outworking of pain in the world that comes from rebellion against the King has an eternal outworking, too: hell, meaning eternal separation from the King of life and love. The two common questions, 'What is the meaning of life?' and, 'What happens when I die?' are answered with assurance and hope through knowing the King. (Acts 3:19-21)

To return to a simple gospel, we must return to a simple truth: God is King. The gospel is the story of how a perfect King could love an imperfect and rebellious people back into his perfect kingdom. It is understandable that people may reject human author- itarianism in this broken world, but they have surely yet to meet the one true perfect King of the universe. It is only because the perfect King exists that we can feel so let down by the imperfect substitutes that jockey for his reign in our lives.

How we present this truth is a matter for further discussion, and we will talk about contextualisation in Chapter Four. So let's wrap things up here with a question: do we have a suitable understanding of the kingdom truth at the heart of the gospel, from which we can share God's hope with the world?

Once again we come back to the core issue raised in Chapter One: to preach simply we must have a sufficiently deep understanding of what the good news really is. William J. Abraham writes:

> Whatever the gospel is, it enters on the inauguration of the kingdom of God in Jesus Christ, crucified and risen from the dead. Hence, the gospel is not first and foremost about a network of moral injunctions, nor about this or that kind of religious experience, nor about the arrival of the church, nor about some scheme of political liberation, nor about some magic formula to gain health and wealth, nor about a quick and easy way to find celestial fire insurance. It is constituted by those extraordinary events in and through Jesus of Nazareth, through which God acted in history by his Holy Spirit to establish his rule in the world.[25]

Circling back to the earlier analogy of swimming the English Channel, perhaps we can start to see the preaching of the kingdom message not as weights around our arms but as a new stroke style. While at first it may look cumbersome and appear difficult to master, it turns out to be the best and most natural way to successfully complete the challenging swim to the other side.

CHAPTER THREE

THE SPIRITUAL GOSPEL

When I get on a long-haul flight, my usual routine is to put in my earphones and attempt to drift into a world of music-induced sleep for the first couple of hours. On a recent flight, though, I broke with convention and, once seated, decided to spend some time reading (actually, I'm not sure scrolling through Instagram counts as reading).

Eventually, the seat next to me was occupied by a young man in his early twenties, and he looked nervous (presumably about flying rather than because he was sitting next to me). As the last passengers were ushered onboard and into their seats, a baby across the aisle began to wail. I don't mean a little bit of crying; we're talking a full-on wail. Think, 'I just watched the end of E.T.' levels of bawling.[26] This is nothing new for me. God, knowing that I find babies a little irritating at the best of times, routinely likes to position me close to crying infants in enclosed spaces, no doubt as part of my process of spiritual refinement.[27]

The young man turned his head towards me and with a look of despair in his eyes said, 'Ugh, looks like we're in for a long flight.' I laughed and agreed that the acoustic situation was unfortunate. Sure enough, this light exchange sparked a conversation and it wasn't long before he was asking me deep and searching questions about life, faith and God. Before we knew it, four hours had – quite literally – flown by.

We spanned everything from the evidences for the existence of God, science, the origins of the universe, moral philosophy, and the supremacy of following Christ above all other worldviews, religions and philosophies. He was a smart guy and genuinely interested in the dialogue (or 'debate' as he kept calling it), but had some reservations about some of the things I was saying.

In actual fact, he had one major reservation, and it's something that is common among those I speak to about faith today: namely, scepticism towards the supernatural.

Christians are sometimes accused of offering a 'God of the gaps'. In other words, we don't have a better way to explain something so we stick God in there. An example of this criticism might go something like this: Historically, we didn't know how the world was created so we simply stated that God did it. But now, science has set us free from the shackles of our imaginations, enlightened our world and made all the sky-fairy believers look silly. We don't need God to fill the gaps anymore, they say.

Not only are believers accused of sticking God in to conveniently fill the gaps in our scientific (or other) knowledge, we are often accused of being anti-intellectual, against reason and evidence. But anyone who reads the Bible carefully will see that such accusations run contrary to the type of faith Christians are called to hold:

> The Bible actually commands us to use reason and evidence. Jesus tells us that the greatest commandment is to 'love the Lord your God... with all your mind.' God speaks through the prophet Isaiah saying, 'Come now, let us reason together.' Peter urges us to 'always be prepared to give an answer.' Paul commands us to 'destroy arguments' that are opposed to the truth of Christianity, and he declares that Christianity is false unless the resurrection of Christ is an historical fact. So Christians don't get brownie points for being stupid or relying on blind faith. They are supposed to know what they believe and why they believe it.[28]

Christianity is not irrational or anti-intellectual. There are sound reasons as to why Christian faith holds up to testing, and can be accepted as the truth. Not all will be persuaded by the arguments, and no-one was ever argued into the kingdom of God, but reasoned dialogue is a helpful tool for evangelism.

However, no matter how reasoned the arguments may be, once we hit the realm of the supernatural, many non-believers will instantly check out, rejecting the supernatural outright, with a predetermined bias against it that is not necessarily based in any rational thinking. This clearly poses a problem when dealing with God, as it is pretty difficult to avoid the supernatural, God-shaped elephant in the room! I'm not here to make a case for better apologetic and rational arguments for the supernatural (although there are good and helpful ones to be made). I'm actually calling us to press into a supernatural *presentation* of the gospel – that is, proclamation of the properly understood gospel in the power of the Spirit.[29]

As we have already explored in this book, a deep understanding of the gospel is important if we are to proclaim it simply and effectively. The next part of our simple gospel jigsaw is found not so much in the content of our message, i.e. *what* is proclaimed, but in *how* it is proclaimed. The preaching of the apostles reveals to us (amongst other things) the imperative to proclaim the good news in the power of the Spirit.[30]

Preaching Peter

The sermons in Acts and the content of the epistles have much to tell us about what the disciples understood the gospel to be.[31] One striking element is a shift of focus away from the direct proclamation of the kingdom, as modeled by Jesus, to preaching Christ himself as the message.[32]

The content of the disciples' preaching was never going to be the same as that of Jesus because, post-cross and resurrection, Jesus' life and the kingdom message he proclaimed became not merely the model for their preaching but the content of it. Preaching the life, ministry, death and resurrection of Jesus *was and is* preaching the kingdom because the apostles already understood the kingdom truth in which the gospel is anchored, and so must we.

So what then was the gospel message of the early church if it wasn't so explicitly expressed in kingdom language?

The most regular and basic elements are these: (1) the proclamation of the resurrection of Jesus; (2) the call for a response to this proclamation, for repentance and faith in this Jesus; (3) the promise of forgiveness, salvation Spirit to those who so respond... Like the proclamation of Jesus, the *kerygma* [proclamation] of

> the Acts sermons issues in a *call for repentance
> and faith*... the call is specifically for faith *in the
> Lord Jesus* (Acts 9:42; 11:17; 14:23; 16:31).[33]

Peter's sermon at Pentecost is a remarkable account
of gospel proclamation (Acts 2:14-41). Although we
surely only have a summary of what he said, it is clear
that he is committed to presenting Christ as crucified
and risen, that Jesus is the only way to salvation,
and that through a direct invitation for the crowd to
repent and put their trust in Jesus as Lord, around
three thousand were saved.[34]

> It is worth reminding ourselves how much
> store these early Christians set by the plain
> proclamation of the 'Jesus Story'. Whether it
> was spoken by the first-generation apostles or
> written by the second-generation evangelists,
> they expected it to be effective, and it is so
> still.[35]

The reason it was (and is) effective is not merely found
in the fact that the first evangelists got the necessary
elements of the gospel message right, although the fact
that there is remarkable consistency in the elements
of the proclaimed gospel message throughout the
New Testament shows that content is clearly very
important. The reason for success is ultimately found

in the most important aspect of Pentecost itself: The Spirit has arrived, and the Spirit is at work.

As insightful and important as the content of Peter's sermon is, we are surely to take note, above all else, that his preaching power is found in the work of the Spirit. Even the great apostle is powerless to actually save anyone, but when the truth of the Jesus story is presented in the power of the Spirit, people are cut to the heart, and lives are reconciled to God. Where there was death, there is suddenly life.

And this is why the supernatural element is so essential to evangelism, because it is not just an awkward inconvenience in the content of our message (the resurrection; the [super]nature of God, etc.), but is the means by which the message comes to life in the heart of the listener – through the Spirit's power.[36] Rather than running scared from a supernaturally sceptical audience, our task is to press into that which some find objectionable until it reveals itself to be true.

When Peter invites his audience to repent and trust in Jesus, let us not forget that he is giving each listener the opportunity to put his message to the test. Come, taste and see that the Lord is good (Ps. 34:8). The true test of the authenticity of the supernatural is found in the transformed heart of a believer. I am not the same as I was before I received the gospel, because God's

Spirit is at work in me. Put your trust in him and see for yourself.

Preaching Paul

Speaking of transformed hearts, there is surely no more striking example than that of Saul of Tarsus. After his encounter with the risen Christ, and once the scales had fallen from his eyes (a great example of the Bible making its point through literal event *and* metaphor in the same instance), Saul became Paul: one of the most significant evangelists to ever have carried the gospel into the world. What can we learn from his proclamation of the gospel?

Paul told the Corinthian believers:

> When I came to you, I did not come with eloquence or human wisdom as I proclaimed to you the testimony about God. For I resolved to know nothing while I was with you except Jesus Christ and him crucified. I came to you in weakness with great fear and trembling. My message and my preaching were not with wise and persuasive words, but with a demonstration of the Spirit's power, so that your faith

might not rest on human wisdom, but on God's power. (1 Cor. 2:1-5, NIV)

Here we see Paul putting into words what we have already seen the apostles outworking through Acts: he is only interested in preaching the Jesus story, and the story must be proclaimed in the power of the Spirit so that it is not merely a set of biographical facts or theological propositions, but a revelation of the way to salvation *and* the means by which salvation is found. It is the way *and* the means to finding peace with the King of the universe, and all the benefits that come with it.

> The form of [Paul's] gospel is indeed similar to that of the Jerusalem church... nevertheless the dynamic for his preaching, the authorisation for it, the conviction about it, came not from any mere knowledge of the events... but from an encounter with the risen Christ himself.[37]

Paul's testimony is one of supernatural encounter and radical transformation. While his gospel message is no doubt influenced by, and rooted in, the Jesus story as told and recorded by his apostolic peers (and his understanding of the gospel is second to none – Peter even found Paul's theology too dense at times!), his conviction for its authority and the truth of its content is found in the supernatural encounter that forever changed his life. Indeed, it is the very same Jesus that Paul encountered on the road to Damascus who commands his followers to go into the world as his witnesses *in the power of the Spirit* (Acts 1:8).

We will look at Paul's preaching a little more in the next chapter, specifically to explore what we can learn from him about contextualisation of the gospel. But based on what we've briefly explored here, there are three simple things that we can discern from the first preachers of the gospel that will impact our evangelism today (the first two directly, and the third by implication):

1. **The elements of the gospel message are important**: Know the Jesus story as the truth about the kingdom of God and learn to express it well to an audience. The life, ministry, death and resurrection of Jesus are the heart of the gospel we proclaim. These facts, properly understood, were of paramount importance to those first evangelists and should likewise be to us today, so we do not fall into the trap of preaching a distortion of the true story and turn the gospel into no gospel at all (Gal. 1:6-7).

2. **Evangelism is impossible without the Spirit's power**: Preaching in the power of the Spirit is the

only way people will truly move from hearing the facts of the Jesus story to recognising that God is knocking on the door of their heart and calling them home. The gospel is the *power of God* to bring salvation to all who believe (Rom. 1:16).

3. **Prayer is essential to evangelism**: If we want God involved then we must devote ourselves to prayer. Prayer for our own relationship and faith. Prayer for opportunities. Prayer for the preparation of hearts to receive the message. Prayer for boldness. Prayer for salvation. Prayer for healing. Prayer for wisdom, discernment, sensitivity.... Prayer is the bedrock of evangelism. Preaching the gospel without prayer is, I believe, the most common reason that our evangelism fails. Prayer doesn't guarantee success of salvation, but it does guarantee that we've put the power in the right hands, and from there, anything is possible (Mt. 9:7-8; Rom. 10:1).

Supernaturally Strengthened

Returning to the story of the young man on the flight, at the end of our conversation he thanked me for taking the time to answer his questions and told me that I had helped him think more deeply about the subjects we had discussed. He then revealed something amazing to me, that he was not in fact supposed to be on the flight. He had overslept and missed his earlier flight so had been rebooked onto the one we now shared. Not only that, but he had rejected two other possible seats before settling on the one he now occupied, and he couldn't explain why.

I smiled at him and said, 'You know, if you believed in the supernatural you might be inclined to believe that this is not a coincidence, and that maybe God is telling you something'. He laughed in appreciation of the irony. I happened to have a new copy of C.S. Lewis' *Mere Christianity* with me and felt prompted to give it to him, along with my contact information so that he could keep in touch via email if he desired. He was genuinely touched by this gesture and said, as we parted ways, 'When I get home I'm going to read this book, and I'm going to pray and ask God if he is really there.' I told him I would be praying for him, and I have been.

I don't know whether he did go home and seek God, but I know that God was beginning to speak to him on that flight (and this serves to remind us that evangelism is not usually an event but a process).[38] I could see that in his attitude and demeanour over the course of the conversation. As we spoke, I was praying constantly that God would minister to his heart and move beyond his scepticism. Hopefully, my answers to his questions were sound and went some way to clearing a pathway to the cross through his objections, but it is the Spirit of God that will move him to a place of true repentance, who will minister to him, day in and day out, if he chooses to truly live for the King.

Many in the world may be anti-supernatural, but our preaching and sharing of the gospel must not be. When we proclaim the Jesus story in the power of the Spirit, even the most sceptical heart can be opened up to the glory of God. The same gospel Peter proclaimed at Pentecost has lost none of its power to save, to move hearts and to change preconceptions. The same Spirit who empowered Peter and Paul to proclaim the Jesus story two thousand years ago is at work today, empowering you for the task that lies before you.

The beautiful irony for preachers who find themselves faced with a supernaturally sceptical audience is that the hope of success is found *in* the supernatural – proclamation of the glorious good news in the power of the Spirit. It is actually profoundly simple, and nothing else will do.

THE CULTURAL GOSPEL

I love movies. So much so that when I decided to go to university there was only one subject I was interested in – Film Studies. During the first week of lectures my professors kept telling the class that the course would change the way we watched films, that going to the movies would never be the same again. Sure enough, I learned a lot about how to 'read' a film (pretentious, don't ask), and my studies have had an impact on my viewing experiences ever since.

In one particular class, we watched a documentary about the impact of certain cultural trends on teenagers and it included a segment about two American teenagers who had supposedly been so negatively influenced by death metal music that they ended up killing a classmate. During group discussion on the subjects raised in the film, my lecturer turned to me, knowing I was a Christian, to see what I thought about the documentary's conclusions about this supposedly 'satanic' music and its influences. He wasn't trying to catch me out, it was a genuine attempt to bring different viewpoints into the discussion, but I was woefully underprepared and a little too enthusiastic to share my views and present something of the gospel to my classmates.

Ten minutes later, and despite the best efforts of my lecturer to protect me from myself in front of the class, I had dug myself a hole of generalisation, overstated opinion, and poorly explained views on the dangers of opening yourself to the demonic. In short, I had made myself look like a bit of a Christian weirdo.[39] I learned two valuable lessons that day. Firstly, there are some amazing opportunities for Christ-centred dialogue that can arise from engaging with movies, media, art, culture, the news, and so on; there was actually a really good conversation to be had off the back of the documentary, which could have left my classmates with some hugely positive spiritual food for thought. Which leads me to the second thing I learned: putting some thought into what you are going to say before you say it is generally a good idea.[40]

Although my university studies left their mark on my viewing habits, nothing has impacted my engagement with movies and pop culture as much as my faith in Jesus. Movies, even purely as entertainment, are always viewed through the lens of my faith, which is the framework through which I make sense of everything in life. In fact, we are all influenced and shaped by the worldviews we inherit and adopt; we all perceive the world around us in light of the worldviews we hold.

Using familiar and popular elements from culture can be a great way to engage people in dialogue about Jesus and begin to address the problems with the worldviews they hold, although – as my university experience revealed – it carries the danger and potential for miscommunication, especially when we are more eager to engage than to understand. For that reason, before we consider engaging with culture for gospel opportunity, it is worth grounding ourselves in the reality that the gospel itself is inherently *counter*-cultural. In our attempt to understand the gospel deeply, for the purpose of simple explanation, this truth is invaluable.

The Counter-Cultural Gospel

It is not possible for the gospel to be subsumed into mainstream culture and still be the gospel. What I mean by that is, when we try to bend and shape the gospel of Jesus Christ to fit into the confines of a specific (human-centred) culture, we will be forced to compromise it in some way. Culture grows out of the thinking, interactions, and applications of (fallen) human beings, within a society (either consciously and intentionally, or subversively), and there will therefore always be elements of any given culture that do not sit in harmony with the gospel.

> The gospel is the lifeblood of Christianity, and it provides the foundation for countering culture. For when we truly believe the gospel, we begin to realise that the gospel not only compels Christians to confront social issues in the culture around us. The gospel actually creates confrontation with the culture around – and within – us.[41]

The gospel isn't just a call to speak out about our cultural concerns, but by its very nature it actually *creates* confrontation by being fundamentally incompatible with certain aspects of human-shaped culture. This 'culture war' actually starts internally, within a person's life. The gospel is an assault on the 'culture of rebellion' that we choose as humans, until we place our trust in Jesus and live for him. That is why the gospel is so offensive to so many, because it directly challenges and calls out the deficiencies of any worldview that is counter to Christ – worldviews that are held so tightly by so many as the full meaning of their existence.[42]

An analogy for this (and returning us to the world of the movies) would be going to see a film and walking out two hours later having fallen in love with what you just experienced on the screen. But then your friend chimes in that the movie wasn't very good and starts listing all of the problems they had with it, and you become defensive. If the film had any kind of emotional impact on you, you may even feel their rejection of the film as a rejection of you and the things you hold dear. If that can happen with a subjective experience, such as deciding how 'good' or enjoyable a film was (and I, for one, take film appraisal very seriously – no-one will ever talk me out of holding *Indiana Jones and The Temple of Doom* up as the greatest film of all time), how much more so can the highlighting of a deficient worldview and culture cause problems between people who disagree about what matters in life?

We had better be sure, when challenging the world-views of those who have not yet put their trust in Jesus, that we understand the worldview we are presenting as the truth (the gospel) in its place. We must also attempt to understand something of the context of the person we are sharing with, in the hope that it might help us shape the way in which we package and deliver the message, that it would be received as clearly as possible.

Re-Packaging The Gospel

When most people talk of contextualising the gospel, they think about it in terms of essentially *re-packaging* the message for a specific audience. For example, using illustrations and analogies to explain the message in a way that connects with people's cultural understanding today. However, the starting point for 'contextual evangelism' is not actually in repackaging the gospel message, but in attempting to understand the context into which we are bringing the good news.

Mission is contextual. That is to say, it always takes place within a context (within a culture). Having some understanding of the culture around you is therefore a crucial step for effective engagement with those you are trying to reach. I was preaching recently at a conference for church pastors from a large Nigerian church denomination in the UK. I was asked to help them think about cross-cultural outreach: how could these pastors reach beyond the African community and impact a wider audience with the gospel? I was delighted by their passion and desire to reach out with the gospel, but had to confess to them that my advice was fairly simple. The key, I told them, to reaching any culture, any people group or worldview that is different to your own, is to listen. The more we listen, the more we understand. The more we understand, the more we can build bridges from the truth of the gospel to the reality of the life of the hearer (and move beyond the barriers and preconceptions that impede the gospel message ever taking root).

I stated in the previous chapter that prayer is the spiritual bedrock of evangelism. Listening to those with whom we share the gospel is pretty high on the list of evangelistic essentials, too. James tells us that we should be quick to listen and slow to speak (Jam. 1:19). Jesus is frequently presented as listening to people throughout the gospels, often asking them questions as he does so, in order to discover more about their needs and concerns, and ultimately to bring revelation of his kingdom truth to bear on their lives.[43] In short, Jesus treated people as people, rather than as evangelistic targets, and so must we.

This is where pop culture can be really helpful, often giving insight into what is considered important and of value within any given society (or what is shaping those values). It can be easy for the church to demonise popular culture and dismiss it too quickly. The over-simple rationale can be: if it's popular in the world, that probably means it's bad. But this doesn't necessarily follow:

> The truth is more complex. There are good and bad pieces of popular culture, just as there are good and bad pieces of high, elite culture... a piece of culture's popularity ought to make

Christians curious why so many find meaning there.[44]

Think about the resurgence of *Star Wars* over the last few years (did it ever really go away?). For some people, *Star Wars* is practically a religious experience that impacts their lives in important ways. I have a friend who is more evangelistic about *Star Wars* than many Christians are about Christ (which may sadly say more about some Christians than anything else…). You might find the idea of spaceships, alien puppets and glowing swords all rather tedious, but you don't need to like *Star Wars* to realise that there is clearly an amazing opportunity to engage with this huge cultural touchstone and create gospel-centred dialogue from it.

To simply dismiss any piece of popular culture as 'immoral', 'unChristian' or 'not my cup of tea' is to miss asking the crucial questions: Why is it so popular? What meaning are people finding within it? What might it teach me about the culture I am trying to effectively reach with the good news?

Using any Christocomplementary (I'm pretty sure I've made this word up, but I like it so let's run with it) aspects within popular culture to the advantage of evangelism (and discipleship, for that matter) is likely an effective way to engage with those who have no framework for Christian reality other than that which you provide, so why not give them some reference they can connect with? Whilst we should press against any counter-Christian elements with wisdom and discernment, it is important not to be blindly dismissive when something within pop culture comes along that is blatantly counter to the gospel. We can *engage* with something without actually *affirming* it.[45]

In short, if the masses are engaging with and being shaped by culture in the marketplace of ideas, then in the same way that Paul used pagan poetry in his explanation of the gospel at Mars Hill (Acts 17:16-34), we should consider engaging with and using the popular culture of our time to reach those who are most impacted by it – that they may ultimately encounter Jesus.[46]

> Paul did not avoid secular culture, ignoring classical texts or philosophy or rhetoric. Nor did Paul confine his learning to Jewish/Biblical topics such that he could lecture on the theology of the book of Psalms but was ignorant of Plato. Paul had studied Greco-Roman literature to some extent, which enabled him to use it when it would help him make a case for the gospel.[47]

Shaping our proclamation and explanation of the gospel message (contextualisation) in light of what we know about culture can be very helpful in connecting listeners to the message, but there are three questions I believe we must ask when attempting to do so:

1. AM I ADDING OR TAKING AWAY ANYTHING FROM THE CORE GOSPEL MESSAGE?

This begs the question that we keep returning to: do you have a sufficiently complex understanding of the gospel from which to work this out? If your repackaging of the gospel is distorting the message through addition to, or subtraction from, the truth of the gospel, you need to rethink your approach.

2. IS THE CONTEXTUALISATION APPROPRIATE/HELPFUL FOR THE SPECIFIC AUDIENCE I AM SPEAKING TO?

Are we making assumptions about what will be helpful cultural touchstones for people? Will explaining the gospel in light of last night's episode of *The Walking Dead* to the eight-year-olds at summer camp really be appropriate? Or how about playing the latest Calvin Harris track as a primer for gospel discussion when invited to speak at a seniors group?[48] Contextualisation is never for its own sake, it is used for one reason alone: to make the message accessible.

3. IS IT REALLY NECESSARY?

We might assume that contextualisation is the same as simplification, but this is not always the case. Sometimes, our illustrations and attempts to build bridges from the gospel to the culture and lives of our listeners can confuse things, even when the cultural reference is appropriate. If your re-packaging of the message is making things more complicated, you don't need it. Keep it simple.

These questions, asked and reflected upon honestly, will help us to discern whether our evangelism is becoming deficient in its content, inaccessible to the audience, or unnecessarily complicated. I am in no way opposed to the idea of contextualisation, but I do firmly believe that presenting the Jesus story, the basic tenets of the gospel, in the power of the Spirit is the primary goal. In my experience, contextualisation works best as a way of gently enhancing the clarity of these basic gospel truths, rather than as a radical reinvention of them.

Experiencing The Gospel

Think about it like this: imagine needing to convince someone who has only ever seen a motorbike, and who laughs at the idea of a four-wheeled vehicle, that there are in fact such things as cars. You could add a sidecar to the motorbike to broaden their thinking from the standard two-wheeled bike, or even build a new chassis around the bike out of cereal boxes, Sellotaping a couple of extra wheels on in the hope that building upon what they already know will help them to grasp the concept.

Or, you could just give them a ride in your car.

Hold on, you're thinking, that doesn't feel like a fair analogy because we *explain* the gospel, whereas the guy in the story gets to tangibly experience the car, to see and touch it. In John's gospel we read the story of the Samaritan woman who, after a transforming encounter with Jesus, returned to her town and implored those she met to, 'Come, see a man who told me everything I've ever done.' (John 4:29, NIV). Perhaps she understood evangelism better than most, for sharing the gospel should never be *mere* explantation, but an offer to come, see and experience for yourself the risen Christ; to take a ride in the car.[49]

Contextual evangelism is not about a radical repackaging of the gospel message, but an attempt to understand what has taken the place of Christ in people's lives (often revealed through pop culture), and to present the gospel in a simple way that speaks to the deficiency of those things, helping people to see that they need not exist in darkness but can live in the light.[50]

As has been reiterated all the way through this book, the deeper our understanding (and application) of the gospel, the more likely it is that we will be able to express simple truths in any context with real integrity, not watering down our content to such a degree that our dialogue ceases to be gospel-centred in any meaningful sense, but so that it maintains its power through simple expression and faithfulness to the task God has set before us (Mt. 28:16-20).

Genuine cultural change will only come as Christians faithfully proclaim and live out this transformational gospel. As we attempt to become all things to all people in order that we might save some (1 Cor. 9:22-23), it would be wise of us to listen to those with whom we desire to share the good news, in order to identify the connection points for the gospel that are already present in their lives. To help us engage effectively, through preaching or personal witness, let's try to wise up to the culture that surrounds us, engaging with it as it currently is, with the aim of pointing people to what God has always intended for it to be, through the power of simple, culturally aware gospel sharing.

THE IDENTITY GOSPEL

In the late eighties, Walt Disney's *Pinocchio* was rereleased in UK cinemas. This is not only my first memory of going to the movies but one of my very earliest memories of anything. Most of the experience has been lost or blurred by time, but two things in particular stand out. Firstly, I remember being somewhat overwhelmed by the epic climax to the film that features our heroes being swallowed by a huge whale. The size and scale of what I was seeing was unlike anything I'd ever experienced before, and it vividly sticks in my mind to this day.

The second memory of that trip to the movies is of standing in the foyer after the film had ended. I can only assume we were waiting for my mum and sister, who must've been off doing mum-and-sister-type things (this is based on observations conducted in clothing stores and shopping malls around the UK over the following years). My dad crouched down to talk to me and the exchange went something like this:

INT. CINEMA FOYER — DAY

A four-year-old boy — BEN — stands in a movie theatre foyer with his dad, having just watched the classic Disney animation, 'Pinocchio'. The dad crouches down to fasten the buttons on his son's coat.

DAD

Wasn't it good at the end when Pinocchio became a real boy!

BEN

(Confused)

What?

DAD

At the end, when he became a real boy.

BEN

(More Confused)

I didn't see that…

DAD

Yes you did. At the end he had real arms and legs instead of wooden ones, remember?

The little boy begins to cry.

DAD

What's the matter?

BEN

(Crying)

I didn't see him become a real boy! I
didn't see it!

Admittedly, as far as classic scenes go it's not exactly *Casablanca*, but this is how the moment played out. My first trip to the movies ended in heartbreak. Somehow, in the excitement of the whole experience I had missed the resolution of the story. In the mind of this four-year-old, Pinocchio was eternally trapped as a wooden boy. Forget about the donkey transformation sequence (which is genuinely scary for a kids' film!), the real horror of the movie for me was that I hadn't experienced the true resolution – I'd missed the whole point of the story.[51]

So many people today live lives that utterly miss the point. Identity is surely the central theme of human existence as we all attempt, in various ways – consciously or otherwise – to make sense of the breath in our lungs and the reality we experience each day. The most basic question a person asks is simply, 'Who am I?' How we answer that question is profoundly important, shaping as it will how we live our lives.

In my view, the greatest problem the world faces is one of an identity crisis. Seeking to find your identity, fulfilment and peace in anything other than that for which you were created – relationship with God – is to miss the point of life, and has catastrophic effects for you and the world you inhabit.

If identity crisis is the great problem of our age, then personal freedom is surely the idol. As we are faced with some of the highest rates we've ever known of suicide, depression, anxiety, self-harm, eating disorders and other such devastation, we must recognise and be stirred by the fact that the identity, worldview and 'freedoms' that so many subscribe to are deeply destructive.[52] As I write this, I am brokenhearted to think of the thousands who will not only contemplate but attempt suicide in the time it takes me to finish this chapter. Oh Lord, would you bring the hope of your true identity to bear on someone in that situation right now. Authentic Jesus followers must resolve to know the identity of Christ and, presenting the truth of who he is to the world, bring hope to the hopeless so that none would miss the point of the gift of life we have been given.

In this chapter and the next, we will explore identity. Here, we will look at the identity of God (and, to give you fair warning, things are going to get a little more complex); then, in the final chapter, we will explore how God's identity impacts our own as we seek to live in the light of who he is.

The Identity of God

'Who do you say I am?' Jesus asked his disciples (Mt. 16:15; Mk. 8:29; Lk. 9:20). This question sits at the heart of the gospel itself – who is Jesus Christ? If the truth claims of the Bible are correct then the answer to this question holds the key to understanding life today, and the eternal hope that lies beyond.

Identity is not only the central theme of human existence but a central theme of the Bible, dealing as it does with the story of God and his creation. The Bible tells us who God is, who we are, how he relates to us and we to him. God is revealed from the very first words of Genesis as the eternal, pre-existent creator of the universe. A question that frequently arises when talking about God as the beginning of all things is, 'Well, who made God then?' The answer is: no-one. After all, if someone created God – we will call this new character Mega God – then he is better than God. I don't want to worship God anymore, I want to worship Mega God! Problem solved, right? But wait, who made Mega God? Super-Mega God?

We inevitably lose ourselves in an infinite cycle of gods creating gods, leaving us with the same predicament: what was the beginning point, the first cause? God has necessarily always existed and is the beginning of all things, including time and space itself. As challenging as it may be to get our minds around this, it is far more plausible to assume an eternally existent creator (for whom time is part of his creation) than to assert the alternative, that *nothing* made *something*. Indeed, it is that very belief that leads so many down a road of hopelessness: we came from nowhere and are going nowhere, so what's the point?

From the opening premise of God as eternal creator, we read on to discover more about him. He is not simply a creator who has finished his work and now sits disinterested in his creation. He is not dead, as Friedrich Nietzsche infamously declared more than a hundred years ago. He is alive and kicking, and we can know him through the teaching of the Bible, the historical person of Jesus Christ, and personal experience (revelation) of his love and truth.

The Bible reveals God to be love itself (1 Jn. 4:16), good (Mk. 10:18), gracious (Rom. 3:23-24), wise (Rom. 11:33), holy (Ex. 15:11), righteous (Ps. 50:6), patient (2 Pet. 3:9), merciful (Mic. 7:18), faithful (2 Tim. 2:11-13), perfect (Ps. 18:30), forgiving (Ex. 34:5-7), compassionate (Ps. 116:5), sovereign (1 Chron. 29:11-12), eternal (Ps. 90:2), a heavenly

Father (Mt. 23:9), just (Isa. 30:18), and so the list goes on and on. The identity of God springs forth from the pages of his holy Word, revealing him to be more than we could dare to hope for.

We also discover, as we read the Bible, that God is one in *essence* and three in *person*: Father, Son and Spirit, or the Holy Trinity (Mt. 28:19; 2 Cor. 13:13-14; 1 Pet. 1:2; Rev. 1:4-6). There is no easy way to describe the Trinity; it is a divine mystery. Analogies always come up short because the idea of three-in-one doesn't make any mathematical sense to us, irrespective of how we reimagine it for the sake of our limited brains. The best I have found is to think of toothpaste with three stripes to it: red, white and blue. Each stripe is the toothpaste, with its own distinctive colour, and yet together they are the same toothpaste. As with others, there are of course holes to be picked in this analogy, but it points us in the right direction. It is important to remember that the three figures of the godhead are equal. To make the Father more than the Son and Spirit would be to err towards unitarianism, and to overemphasise the distinctiveness of the three takes us dangerously close to polytheism (multiple gods).

We must simply understand and accept God as he is presented biblically, as an undivided unity expressed in threefold nature: Father, Son, Spirit. This is important because it tells us that God has always existed in relationship with himself. God creates out of the eternal relationship of the Trinity for a future eternal relationship with the human beings of his creation. When this relationship becomes broken because of our rebellion against God, the three persons of the Trinity work as one to give us the hope of the gospel. Salvation is a Trinitarian event, initiated by the Father, implemented by the Son, and applied by the Spirit.[53]

Let's turn our attention to the identity of Jesus. If we want to help people answer the question, 'Who is Jesus Christ?' we need to understand, as deeply as possible, the man that stepped out of heaven two thousand years ago to undertake the greatest rescue mission in the universe, and in the process became the visible image of the invisible God (Col. 1:15).

Messiah

'You are the Messiah, the Son of the living God,' Peter declares, in response to Jesus' identity question (Mt. 16:16, NIV). You've likely heard the word Messiah before, but you may not actually know what it means. The Hebrew word means 'anointed one' (*Christos* in the Greek, from which we get *Christ*). It is not reserved exclusively for Jesus, but was in fact a title of honour, usually given to the high priest and the king.[54]

That being said, those who lived in Jesus' day had all sorts of ideas about a specific figure known as 'the Messiah'. These ideas were pretty much always related to the concept of a saviour. The average Jew who heard the title would almost certainly have had in mind the rising up of a king from the line of King David, who would save Israel in the end of days, releasing them from the pain of being ruled by foreign invaders (in the first century, the Romans), and securing full independence for them to live and worship freely in their true identity as the people of God, for all time (2 Sam. 7:11-17).[55]

Another word that is worth unpacking is 'anointed'. Anointing is actually central to the concept of messiahship; for example, priests had to be anointed (a kind of commissioning, usually by applying oil) to conduct their duties (Lev. 4:3, 5, 16) and with the anointing came the power from God himself for the task at hand.[56] However, God needs no anointing for he holds *ultimate* authority and power, derived exclusively from himself (Ps. 2, 18, 20, 21, 22, 89, 101, 139).

When Peter declares that Jesus is the Messiah, he is saying something hugely significant, along the lines of: 'You are the King, the empowered one of heaven by God's appointment, the Saviour sent to rescue God's people'. While Peter surely doesn't yet understand the full implications of Jesus' messiahship, he (and the other disciples on whose behalf he is speaking) recognises that Jesus is *more* than the earthly king who will reclaim Jerusalem by force. This is evident in the fact that he doesn't stop with the word 'Messiah'. What tumbles from his mouth next is astonishing, as he declares that Jesus is 'the Son of the living God'.

How then had the disciples arrived at this audacious truth?

> It is unlikely that this is the first occasion on which the apostles thought of Jesus as Messiah… it was because they saw Jesus in this capacity that they left their homes and followed him. But as they lived and worked with him, their understanding of 'Messiah' enlarged.[57]

Son of Man

We don't need to look too deeply into the words and deeds of Jesus' life to see that his journey with the disciples was one big flashing neon sign that declared a simple truth – the King of Peace is here to save the world.

You can learn a lot about a person from how they talk about themselves, the nicknames they choose to adopt, and what they affirm that others have said about them. Jesus doesn't deny that he is the Messiah or the Son of the living God when Peter declares it. Instead, he defers back to his own favoured title for himself: Son of Man. Jesus used this title more than eighty times in the New Testament, and is the only person to use the term of himself. That should be of note to us, until we realise that the title 'Son of Man' really just means a human man. So Jesus' favourite way to title himself was, basically, 'a bloke'?

Actually, the story of Jesus forgiving and healing the paralysed man in Mark 2 will help us figure out why this term is so important in helping the disciples (and us) discover and understand Jesus' identity. Jesus is accused of blasphemy by the teachers of law for offering the forgiveness of sins, which is something that only God has the authority to do. Jesus, in one of the more rock-and-roll demonstrations of his kingdom identity, both affirms verbally that the Son of Man has authority to forgive sins and then *confirms* this authority in the most powerful way possible, through the miracle of healing that follows.

Jesus' specific use of the term 'Son of Man' here[58] means that not *all* humans can forgive sin, but he can. He is like no other human; he is unique because he possesses an authority unlike any other: he possesses the authority of God.

Okay, we might be getting a bit technical for a book about *simplicity*, but this is important stuff so stay with me. Let me try to explain the importance of this story in three points:

1. IT REVEALS A DIRECT CLAIM OF DIVINE IDENTITY.

I have sometimes heard people say that Jesus never claimed to be God. They must be reading a different New Testament to me because it seems like almost everything Jesus does is either a direct or indirect claim of his divinity. The story of the forgiveness and healing of the paralytic man is one example, but everywhere we turn in the Jesus story we see claims of divine identity:

- His use of the name of God (I AM) for himself, almost getting him stoned for blasphemy by the Pharisees, who clearly knew what he meant (Jn. 8:58-59), and in response to the direct question of his messianic identity by the Sanhedrin (Mk. 14:62).

- His claim to be the fulfilment of Scripture (Lk. 4:16-21; Lk. 10:23-24).

- His self-centred teaching, calling people to himself (Jn. 11:25; Jn. 14:6).

- His association with God the Father: 'I and the Father are one.' (Jn. 10:30; Mt. 11:27).

- His claim to judge the world (Mt. 25:31-46).

- His unique authority to teach the truth: 'When Jesus had finished saying these things, the crowds were amazed at his teaching, because he taught as one who had authority, and not as their teachers of the law.' (Mt. 7:28-29; Jn. 6:47, NIV)

This is only the briefest overview of Jesus' divine claims, but be under no illusions: Jesus claimed to be God in what he said and revealed himself to be as such in the things he did, not least in his resurrection.[59]

2. IT REVEALS JESUS AS FULLY MAN AND FULLY GOD.

That most mind-bending of realities (well, alongside the Trinity!) that Jesus was one hundred percent man and one hundred percent God, at the same time, is revealed in the title 'Son of Man'. He wants us to know that he is indeed a human being (the literal meaning of the term), but that he is unique amongst humans as he is the anointed one of heaven, the suffering servant of Isaiah 53, the saving King prophesied in 2 Samuel, the eternal judge who will return as one like a 'Son of

Man', coming on the clouds of heaven at the end time to rule and reign forever (Dan. 7:13-14). He is the fulfilment of all Scripture, the hope for all humanity.

3. IT REVEALS THE EVANGELISTIC IDEAL OF WORD AND DEED MINISTRY.

Jesus reveals the truth of his claims to authority through his actions; in this example, the forgiveness of sin is accompanied by the healing miracle. Jesus has authorised us to do likewise in the world: to speak out his truth and to use his spiritual power to live a life that matches up to what we preach (Gal. 5:22-25), and to see signs and wonders, such as healings, effected in the world today.

The disciples recognised Jesus' messianic identity through his ministry and in his self-designated title, 'Son of Man'. Thomas' declaration, upon meeting the resurrected Jesus, that he is 'My Lord and my God' (Jn. 20:28) leaves us in no doubt that by the time Jesus ascended to heaven, the disciples knew exactly who he was. Ultimately, they worshipped him as Messiah, the King of kings, and their worship – as the climax of his life, death and resurrection – is the strongest evidence of his true identity.

[I]t is absurd to postulate complete discontinuity between the ministry of Jesus and the worship of Christ. If during his lifetime Jesus had never intimated that He was the Son of God, it would be very strange that His followers worshiped Him in that capacity after His death.[60]

The moment I missed in *Pinocchio* as a kid was the moment the puppet became a real boy. When the world misses that the pre-existent King Jesus stepped into the world and became a real human boy, it misses the most important moment in all of history – God became man, dwelt among us, revealed his identity, died and rose again that we would know our true identity and receive life, and life eternal. If you want to know the point of life, you need to know the one who made life, the one who came to give you life in all its fullness (Jn. 10:10).

The title the disciples would eventually use for their King would not be his preferred 'Son of Man', but the name by which he is still known around the world two thousand years later:[61]

Jesus *Christ*.

His name now fully reveals his identity. He *is* The Messiah. He *is* the Anointed One. The King has come.

CHAPTER SIX

THE INTENTIONAL GOSPEL

During my early career as a DJ I spent many weekends playing in bars and clubs. For me, this was always ministry, an attempt to use my DJ skills (limited as they were) to reach out to those on the party scene. After DJing in one particular bar for a few months and getting to know the staff well, I remember a specific night when the bar owner came up to the booth to see how it was going.

In the small hours of the morning, and as I was in full flow, mid-mix, he leaned over to me and said, 'So what's all this God stuff about then?'. Taken by surprise, I was completely thrown and made a total hash of the mix. No problem though, there were more important things at stake, and we spent the next ten minutes chatting about faith in Jesus. And that was that. He walked away that night, thoughtful about some of the things I had said, and for the rest of the time I performed in his bar, it never really came up again.

Fast forward a few years and I was back in that same city to once again play in one of the club venues. Once I'd finished my set it was late and I wanted to get on with the two-hour drive back home so I made a move to leave the club. But on my way out I bumped into the same bar owner from years before, who had just popped into the club with some friends. I spent some time chatting with him and he filled me in on his life over the last few years. I listened as he told me some of the struggles he had experienced, the regrets he had over failed relationships and opportunities, and a general dissatisfaction with his current circumstances. After lending a sympathetic ear (with one eye on the clock), I told him it was good to see him and went on my way.

Driving home along the dark country lanes that night I had an uneasy feeling in my spirit, and yet I couldn't figure out what it was exactly. And then, the realisation came. Here had been a perfect opportunity to share hope, value, purpose, meaning and love with someone who needed to hear the wonder of the gospel, and I had been more interested in getting home.

I'm not sure I've ever so spectacularly missed an opportunity for the gospel as this. Sure, there have been other occasions when I've sadly failed to be faithful to the witnessing opportunity, but this was long-game stuff. Here was a relationship that had been primed years earlier, and I am convinced that this chance meeting was God-given. I have prayed for him many times since then, that God would let us connect again, or send someone else to share Jesus with him.

You can't really 'accidentally' share the gospel, there has to be some intentionality. Of course there are the occasions, as above, where circumstances align and an unexpected (yet God-given) opportunity presents itself in which it would be harder *not* to share the gospel than to do so. But even in these moments, there still needs to be intentionality, for even the easiest opportunity, handed to you on a plate, can be missed or ignored. Sadly, I walked away from it that night.

Having spent time getting to grips with the identity of Jesus in the previous chapter, it falls to these final pages to bring us home with an affirmation of our own identity *in* Christ and what that means for how we live out the gospel.

An Inconvenient Gospel

The gospel is an inconvenient truth for many. Moving from 'rebellion to reverence' is the core message of the evangelist (Mk. 1:15). Yet, for many, the idea of changing anything about the comfort, independence and personal freedoms of their life is too much to concede.[62] If you are more comfortable with the identity you have (or the one you desire) than the identity presented by the gospel, you are unlikely to accept and submit to the truth claims of the Bible.

Time and time again, God inconveniences people. Look at Abraham and Sarah: having finally been blessed with the son they so desperately wanted, Abraham is then asked to take him up a mountain for a spot of child sacrifice. Inconvenient.

Then there's Moses, happily living out his days with his wife and enjoying the simple life of a shepherd. Then God decides to ignite some shrubbery and Moses finds himself heading back to the land he fled as a murderer to demand that Pharaoh set his entire slave workforce free. Inconvenient.

Esther found favour with the king of Persia after an ancient version of the Miss Universe competition, and became his most celebrated queen, whilst keeping her nationality a secret from him. But then God asks her to risk instant beheading by stepping into the king's presence to inform him of a plot to wipe out her people, the Jews. Inconvenient.

Job is visited by trial after trial, heartbreak after heartbreak, as Satan tries to prove, with God's permission, that it is only those in comfort who will stay faithful in worship. Inconvenient.

The unmarried, teenage Mary is told by an angel that she is pregnant with the Saviour of the world, in a culture that was a little trigger happy when it came to stoning adulterers. Inconvenient.

The spirit-filled evangelist Stephen is snared by a trap and dragged before the Sanhedrin to explain his beliefs, knowing that to represent for Christ will surely lead to his death. Inconvenient.

What do all these people have in common? Faithfulness despite inconvenience. These are all stories of worship.

Abraham was ultimately spared from having to sacrifice Isaac. God provided a substitute for him and suitable worship was offered (Gen. 22:13-14). Moses led the people out of Egypt, God made a way for them to safety so that they could worship him, and the first thing they did upon crossing the Red Sea was to sing a song of praise (Ex. 15:1-21). Esther's story ended not in beheading, but in feasting, joy, happiness and celebration over the salvation of the Jewish people as God used one woman to save many (Est. 8:16-17). Job wrestled over his circumstances but continued to say, 'May the name of the Lord be praised' through it all, and God brought rich restoration to his life (Job 1:21). Mary responded to the news of her pregnancy not with despair and fear but with a song of joy and submission to God, who blessed her abundantly (Lk. 1:46-51). Stephen doesn't condemn those who are stoning him to death but asks God to forgive them, before entering into the eternal inheritance that God has purchased for him through Jesus (Acts 7:59-60).

It is easy to turn the biblical figures into super-humans but, guess what, they were ordinary people like you and me. What made them extraordinary was their choice to trust God, even when life got incon-venient; to worship him even when the circumstances might have prompted them to do otherwise. The Bible tells us that God isn't looking for superheroes, but his eyes are roaming the earth to find a faithful servant who is willing to be inconvenienced, who he can strengthen for the task (2 Chr. 16:9). He's looking for ordinary people who will stand up and say, 'Here I am Lord, send me' (Is. 6:8). While it is good to recognise and celebrate the faith of these wonderful people of God, the glory in these stories does not belong to them. They were faithful, but look again at the outcomes: did you miss it the first time? Here is the same paragraph with some sections in bold to make it clearer:

Abraham was ultimately spared from having to sacrifice Isaac. **God provided a substitute** for him and suitable worship was offered (Gen. 22:13-14). Moses led the people out of Egypt, **God made a way for them** to safety so that they could worship him, and the first thing they did upon crossing the Red Sea was to sing a song of praise (Ex. 15:1-21). Esther's story ended not in beheading, but in feasting, joy, happiness and celebration over the salvation of the Jewish people as **God used one woman to save a people** (Est. 8:16-17). Job wrestled over his circumstances but continued to say, 'May the name of the Lord be praised' through it all, and **God brought rich restoration** to his life (Job 1:21). Mary responded to the news of her pregnancy not with despair and fear but with a song of joy and submission to **God, who blessed her abundantly** (Lk. 1:46-51). Stephen doesn't condemn those who are stoning him to death but asks God to forgive them, before entering into the **eternal inheritance that God has purchased for him through Jesus** (Acts 7:59-60).

There is only one hero in the Bible: God himself. His faithfulness, alone, is perfect. In fact, Paul teaches us that even when we are unfaithful, God remains faithful because it is the very nature of who he is (2 Tim. 2:11-13). Yet he is calling us to faithful lives that are available for service, whatever the cost. He wants to use you as part of his mission in the world. He doesn't do it begrudgingly, he *delights* in using you and empowers you for the task.

Intentional Worship

Willingness and availability are actually all that God asks of you. Are you willing to submit to his Lordship and are you available to be used for his service? Being a Christian means intentionally choosing Christ in every moment of every area of your life, including when it is inconvenient, painful and challenging. This is what it means to take up your cross and follow him (Mt. 10:38), to become a new creation (1 Cor. 5:17), to worship the Father in spirit and truth (Jn. 4:23). This is what it means to be a disciple.

So how do we live as intentional followers of Jesus? Well, the following four commitments are a great place to start:

1. INTENTIONALLY DEVOTIONAL

Devotion is everything. Prayer and study of God's word in the secret place, as well as fellowship with other believers, is the foundation upon which our faith is developed. Spouses who do not talk with each other become distant, and athletes who do not feed their bodies with the right nutrients become ineffective. Devotion keeps our relationship with God living and active, refines us to become like Christ, and fuels us for service (Mk. 1:35).

2. INTENTIONALLY ACCOUNTABLE

God created us out of his eternal triune relationship, for relationship. We are not supposed to live this life in isolation; we are to be connected to our God and to each other. Having trustworthy people in our lives, with whom we journey and to whom we are accountable, helps us to live a holy life that honours God. Accountability is an essential element of holy living: confessing our sins before God, but also to each other. Only God can forgive you, but your close friends can encourage, support, challenge, cry and celebrate with you through the ups and downs of life, if you are prepared to be honest, open and transparent (Jam. 5:16).

3. INTENTIONALLY VERBAL

When Peter and John were hauled before the Sanhedrin for healing in the name of Jesus, they were given a solid and stern warning that they must stop preaching about Jesus. These 'unschooled, ordinary men,' standing in the very place where Jesus was charged with blasphemy by the Jewish authorities, stay firm and simply state that they could never stop talking about what they have seen and heard. They have experienced Jesus, they know the truth, and nothing could stop them sharing this gospel with any who would have ears to hear. Intentionally speaking about who Jesus is and what he has done as a normal part of our lives will build our trust in Jesus, and reveal his glory to the world. Worship music is great, but if you want to take your worship to the next level, start speaking about what he has done for you to anyone who will listen (Acts 4:13, 18-20).

4. INTENTIONALLY SACRIFICIAL

Are there things in your life that are getting in the way of your identity in God? God is not a party-pooper, he has no intention of spoiling your human experience; rather, he desires to protect and affirm what it should always have been. Where you identify distraction – or worse, idolatry – in your life, get rid of it and ask God to help you to be fulfilled in him and transformed by the renewing of your mind (Rom 12:1-2).

All who have breath in their lungs exist, but only those who know Jesus Christ truly live. Jesus has made it possible, through his life, ministry, death and resurrection, for humanity to throw off the shackles of mere existence (which ultimately leads to death) and have a second chance at true life. The gospel is God's *intentional* masterplan for moving an imperfect humanity into relationship with a perfect God, from rebellious existence into true life, to escape hell and enter heaven.

Heaven and Hell, Peace and Chaos

Oh dear, I've mentioned the 'hell' word. Hell makes people uncomfortable, and so it should. Here is the sobering truth though: those who do not put their trust in Jesus Christ are going to hell. It gives me no pleasure to write those words and it may well be inconvenient to talk about hell these days, but if we are serious about helping people escape that awful destiny we cannot hide it away or be embarrassed by it.

One of the most common questions I am asked is, 'Why does a good God allow suffering in the world?' It's an important and fair question. What people are really asking, though, without knowing it is, 'Why is there chaos instead of peace?' Deep down, we all believe that peace, justice and righteousness are the correct way of things. We have a sense of what is fair and unfair, right and wrong, that transcends how we have been raised.

God allows the chaos because true love is always a choice. He will not make us love him, but makes it possible to receive and respond to his love. When we love him, we accept peace (perfection). When we do not, we embrace chaos (imperfection). Our rebellion against God is sin, and this sin has brought death, pain, suffering and chaos to the world. God has begun to put things right by empowering those who love him to be part of the solution in the world, where they were once part of the problem. We become God's ministers of peace and reconciliation into the world when we accept the gospel and live it out. One day, Jesus will return as the King of Peace to restore the perfect kingdom of peace (heaven) for all time, and all who have trusted in him will inherit this kingdom for all eternity. They have been saved from the alternative: eternal chaos in hell.

The Bible does not support the idea of annihilation: that those who die cease to exist, either immediately or after a period of suffering. Neither does it support universalism, where all will ultimately be saved, as much as we might want it to (Dan. 12:2; Mt. 25:46; Mk. 9:48; Jn. 5:28-29; Acts. 24:14-15; Rev. 20:12–15). The Bible affirms two definitive and opposite eternal destinations: those who trust in the Lord Jesus Christ will inherit his kingdom of peace, while those who continue in rebellion will enter the eternal chaos.[63]

Ultimately I don't know exactly what hell will be like, except that it is an eternity of separation from God and is an appalling reality.[64] It is the exact opposite of what the perfectly good and loving God desires for you.[65] It is not good, it lasts forever, and there is no escape once you are there.

The good news is that, while hell is real, noone needs to go to there. Salvation has been made possible for all who put their trust in Jesus. Repent, Jesus declares, you are going the wrong way, you are heading for hell! But he has made the way by which you can live in the kingdom of peace, in perfect eternal relationship with your God.

> Salvation is found in no one else, for there is no other name under heaven given to men by which we must be saved. (Acts 4:12, NIV)

John Stott writes: 'Before we can begin to see the cross as something done for us, we have to see it as something done by us.'[66]

The cross is the centrepiece of the gospel. Without it, there is no Christian faith and there is no hope of salvation. When Jesus died on the cross, he took our sin upon himself (2 Cor. 5:21), bearing our sin that by his wounds we could be healed (1 Pet. 2:24). The cross is complicated, controversial and mysterious. Yet, the basic idea of what Jesus achieved for all through his death and resurrection is surprisingly simple – where there was death, there can now be life. Upon the cross, Jesus atoned (made amends) for our sin, trading the inheritance of our rebellion (eternal death) for the inheritance of his divine identity (eternal life). Because of the cross, God credits our sin to Jesus, and credits Jesus' righteousness to us when we accept him as Lord

(Rom. 10:9). You won't find a better trade than that this side of eternity.

People sometimes ask, 'Can God really forgive me for the things that I've done?' Well, it was your (and my) rebellion that nailed Jesus to the cross, and yet God forgives you for the death of his son (Eph. 4:32). If he can forgive you for that, he can forgive you for anything! When we seek forgiveness in light of what Jesus has done on the cross, God wipes the slate clean (Rom. 8:1-2; Eph. 1:7-8; Col. 1:13-14; 1 Jn. 1:9). There is nothing that can't be forgiven, nothing that can't be put right, if we repent with a sincere heart.

There are those who struggle with the idea of God 'taking it out' on Jesus – something that they see as wrong – or who wrestle over the 'injustice' of an innocent paying the price on behalf of the guilty. Here, again, we are reminded of the importance of under-standing the identity of God and his gospel on a deep level so as to avoid adopting misleading and unhelpful ideas. For example, knowing the Trinity as a perfect unity reveals the fundamental misunderstanding in the idea that God 'takes it out' on Jesus; rather, he offers himself as the way by which the eternally significant realities of the atonement can be achieved, through the cross and the resurrection. Properly understood, the reality of Jesus as our substitute does not leave us with a useless caricature of an angry, petulant God who needed to be arbitrarily appeased, but of a

God of love. A God moved to righteous fury by the evil that humanity chooses – evil that puts an eternal blockage between God and humanity in the form of the barrier of sin that prevents a person from inheriting their place in the perfect kingdom.[67] There is no greater cause for anger or distress to God, and there is no greater response to that anger than to offer *himself* as our perfect substitute:

> 'It cannot be emphasised too strongly that God's love is the source, not the consequence, of the atonement... God does not love us because Christ died for us; Christ died for us because God loved us. If it is God's wrath that needed to be propitiated, it is God's love that did the propitiating... Thus God took his own loving initiative to appease his own righteous anger by bearing it his own self in his own Son when he took our place and died for us. There is no crudity here to evoke our ridicule, only the profundity of holy love to evoke our worship.'[68]

There are various dynamics of the atonement, expressed through fancy theological words such as propitiation, expiation, justification, redemption – and many more – that we could discuss until the end of time. Studying the Word will help you discover more about these important aspects of God's saving work and I encourage you to do so, but as you do, don't lose sight of the central reality of Jesus' death and resurrection, which can be simply expressed: through these events we can be saved from our rebellion, and the barrier to forgiveness and relationship with God can finally be removed if we repent and turn back to him. We can now truly live because of what Jesus has done.

> Salvation in its full sense is from the guilt of sin in the past, the power of sin in the present, and the presence of sin in the future. Thus, while in foretaste believers enjoy salvation now, they still await its fullness (Mark 14:61-62; Heb. 9:28).[69]

Many live in hell during this life. The chaos they experience is horrendous. Jesus calls us all to bring our burdens to him, our worries, fears, struggles and pain, and he will give us rest (Mt. 11:28-30). More significantly, he asks us to bring our sin before him, to seek forgiveness for our sins that put him upon the cross. And forgive us he does. He sets us free to live freely in the grace of the Father's love, with the promise that one day all will be made perfect, as it was when he first created. No more tears, no more pain, no more chaos. Until then, he calls us to go and tell as many as we can that they can know peace instead of chaos (Mt. 28:16-20).

I was recently evangelising to a group of students and I invited questions at the end. A young Muslim woman put her hand up and asked me why God would humiliate himself, lower himself, to become a mere man. The idea was scandalous to her, that the mighty God of all creation would do such a thing. I smiled at her, thanked her for her question and then gave her the only answer I could: the reason, I said, is because that's how much he loves you.

It was staggeringly *inconvenient* for Jesus to lay aside his crown of glory for a crown of thorns, to step from the perfection of heaven into the chaos of the world. Yet this is what he did, for he would rather be inconvenienced by becoming subject to human suffering, the torturous death of the cross, mockery, scorn, humiliation and the taking upon himself of all the sin of humanity, than to see you doomed to eternity in hell.

I'll say it again, the only way to explain why God did what he did is simply this: that's how much he loves you.

I was speaking at a Christian youth conference recently, held in a large convention centre. The staff team at the venue were not Christians and were intrigued by the lively youth gathering they were hosting. I got chatting to one of them, a young guy called Tim, and asked him whether they'd ever seen anything like this in their venue before. They hadn't, and he wanted to know what it was all about. We chatted for a while, and then I let him get back to work!

I couldn't shake him from my mind, so the next day I tracked him down again. I found him cleaning one of the toilets and asked him if he had time to chat once he had finished his work. Ten minutes later he came and met me at the back of the venue. By this time, some of the young people were receiving prayer to be set free from depression and anxiety. We began to talk about this and he revealed to me that he had been struggling with depression. I offered to pray for him and he accepted. While we were praying, he felt the presence of God in a powerful way and stepped back from me saying, 'Woah, what's that I'm feeling?' I told him that it was the Holy Spirit at work and we continued to pray. After this I shared the gospel with him, explaining who Jesus is and what he has done. I simply asked him at the end of this, 'Do you want to live? Do you want to make Jesus Lord of your life?' With tears in his eyes and complete conviction in his voice, he said, 'Yes, I want life. I want Jesus.'

How will the world know that there is salvation, Paul asks in Romans 10, unless we go and preach? Be it from a platform, or in a one-to-one conversation, beautiful are the feet of those who bring good news

– the Jesus story, presented as clearly as we know how, in the power of the Spirit, so that the world will know. Whether those who we speak to make the choice to declare that Jesus Christ is Lord, and to live for him, is not our responsibility, but that they would know the way by which they can be saved surely is. Evangelism is the business of every true follower of Jesus Christ.

Tim went to work the weekend of the youth conference with no idea he was going to encounter the risen King of the universe. Through a simple offer to pray for him and an opportunity seized to share the truth of the Jesus story, he is now alive in Christ. He will inherit the eternal kingdom of peace instead of hell, and God graciously and wonderfully allowed me to be part of the story! God wants to use you to rescue more people like Tim – to reach your family, friends, colleagues, and the stranger in the street.

This whole book can be summed up quite simply (which is helpful for a book that hinges on the idea of simplicity). Who do you say Jesus Christ is? If your answer is that he is who he claimed to be – the King of the universe – then submit to him as Lord. Resolve to know his gospel deeply, to live and share it simply, whatever the cost, so that all may know the hope of his identity, to inherit their place in the eternal kingdom that has been bought for them by his sacrifice.

My favourite hymn is *When I Survey The Wondrous Cross*, the words of which are a perfect anthem to send us out into the world with the hope of the gospel:

When I survey the wondrous cross
on which the prince of glory died
My richest gain I count but loss
and pour contempt on all my pride.

Forbid it, Lord, that I should boast,
Save in the death of Christ my God!
All the vain things that charm me most,
I sacrifice them to His blood.

See from His head, His hands, His feet,
Sorrow and love flow mingled down!
Did e'er such love and sorrow meet,
Or thorns compose so rich a crown?

Were the whole realm of nature mine,
That were an offering far too small
Love so amazing, so divine,
Demands my soul, my life, my all.[70]

Love so amazing, so divine, demands your soul, your life, your all. Will you let him have it?

THE GOSPEL

- You are not an accident. You are created by and in the image of the perfect and loving God (Father, Spirit, Son) who is the source and sustainer of life (Gen. 1).

- All have rejected God (sinned) by going our own way, instead of being obedient to the kind of living our creator intends for us. This is why the world is broken and full of suffering. This injustice angers God who does not trivialise sin by ignoring or excusing it, but who justly punishes those who offend (Rom. 3:23).

- We are powerless to put things right once we have rebelled against God, an act of treason against the King of the universe. Rejection of God (Life) is rejection of Life (God). We are left with eternal death, the natural outworking of our rejection of life *and* of God's punishment (divine justice) for breaking his standard for right living (Rom. 6:23).

- But God desires for none to know death, for he is Love itself and he wants to be in eternal relationship with us, his dearly loved children. God graciously set in motion a rescue mission to save us (1 Tim. 2:4-6).

- God sent his Son, Jesus Christ, into this world as a human being, to live the perfect human life that never rejected the Father God. Jesus was killed upon a cross, acting as our substitute and taking upon himself the death we deserved for our rejection of God (Jn. 3:16; Rom. 3:23–25).

- Three days later, Jesus rose from the dead for he is God, showing that the curse of death is broken. New life is possible *only* through trust in Jesus Christ and the seeking of forgiveness for sin (Prov. 28:13; Eph. 2:1-10; 1 Jn. 1:7-9).

- Jesus' death and resurrection achieved reconciliation, redemption, propitiation (appeasement), and the defeat of evil. Our sin was credited to Jesus, and his righteousness is credited to us (imputed righteousness). The only requirement on our part for this transaction to take effect is that we trust in Jesus as Lord (faith), and believe that God raised him from the dead. We are saved by faith alone. (Mt. 20:28; Rom. 10:9; 2 Cor. 5:18–21; Jn. 12:31; Col. 2:15).

• We can now access a restored relationship with our heavenly Father God. We have peace and are adopted into God's family. We die to our old life and are born again into the new life. (Lk. 9:23; Col.1:20, 2:13-14; Rom. 5:1–2; Gal. 4:4-7).

• Jesus returned to heaven, where he reigns at the right hand of the Father, but he has left believers the gift of the Holy Spirit to empower us to live obediently in the fullness of life, and to help us share the good news with the world. We become new creations, disciples, transformed by the work of the Spirit in our lives, which leads to fruit-fulness. We work as God's ambassadors in the world, representing the kingdom of peace in word and deed, being witnesses to the truth of the Jesus story in word and deed (Mic. 6:8; Acts 1:8; 2 Cor. 5:11-21; Gal. 5:22-23).

• One day, Jesus will return to judge the living and the dead. God's perfect kingdom will be restored and eternal life (heaven) with our loving Father God awaits those who trust in Jesus as Lord. Eternal death (hell) awaits those who do not. The good news is that noone needs to perish eternally;

all can know eternal life and joy in relationship with God, through faith in Jesus Christ (1 Cor. 15; Rev. 21:1-8; 22:1-5).

DISCUSSION
QUESTIONS

Chapter One

1. How well do you think you understand what the gospel is?

2. In what ways does the gospel speak into the complexity of this world?

3. How might longing and desire reveal that the temporary and material life is not all there is?

4. What does it really mean to preach the gospel simply?

5. How can we understand the gospel more fully?

Chapter Two

1. Do you recognise anti-authoritarianism within your culture?

2. How would you explain the gospel in kingdom terms?

3. What are the challenges of the kingdom message today?

4. How might prioritising the message of the kingdom help our gospel preaching and disciple making?

5. How important is an exploration of Jesus' preaching for our own today?

Chapter Three

1. Why might contemporary audiences struggle with the supernatural element of our faith?

2. What does it mean to share the gospel in the power of the Spirit?

3. Why might the preaching of Peter and Paul differ in some ways from that of Jesus?

4. How important is prayer to the task of preaching the gospel?

5. What does your own prayer life look like in relation to your evangelism and preaching?

Chapter Four

1. What is your attitude to and engagement with popular culture?

2. What examples can you think of that show how cultural values are revealed through popular culture today?

3. How might a willingness to engage with popular culture impact your evangelism?

4. How does culture shape the sharing of the gospel?

5. How does the gospel confront the culture around you today?

Chapter Five

1. What are the things that cause people to miss the point of life?

2. How does it change the value and meaning of life if God created the world, or if he did not?

3. How would you, simply but meaningfully, describe the identity of God?

4. What is your response to Jesus' question, 'Who do you say I am?'

5. How could you present this same question to someone this week?

Chapter Six

1. Are you intentional in your evangelism?

2. How has God revealed his faithfulness to you?

3. How might you need to get intentional about your relationship with Jesus?

4. How do we explain the reality of hell to those we witness to, in a loving way?

5. Are you prepared to give your all to Jesus, and what might this look like?

RECOMMENDED FURTHER READING

Evangelism

Honest Evangelism, Rico Tice
The Gospel and Personal Evangelism, Mark Dever
Evangelism and the Sovereignty of God, J.I. Packer
Questioning Evangelism, Randy Newman & Lee Strobel
Power Evangelism, John Wimber

The Gospel

The Cross of Christ, John Stott
Simply Good News, Tom Wright
Scandalous, D.A. Carson

The Empty Cross of Jesus, Michael Green
Whatever Happened To The Gospel, R.T. Kendall
The Good News We Almost Forgot, Kevin DeYoung
The Gospel as Centre, D.A. Carson and Timothy Keller
(eds.)

Christian Belief

Basic Christianity, John Stott
Concise Theology, J.I. Packer
Christian Theology: An Introduction, Alistair McGrath

Apologetics

Confident Christianity, Chris Sinkinson
Mere Apologetics, Alistair McGrath
Mere Christianity, C.S. Lewis
The Reason for God, Tim Keller

ACKNOWLEDGEMENTS

Thanks to those who read the manuscript and offered encouragement and feedback, particularly Joe Boston. I cannot overstate how helpful you have been.

To Andy and The Message family: thank you for entrusting Advance to me and for your constant encouragement and support. I hope and pray that this book will be a valuable tool to believers who share our heart for the lost, to begin to inspire and equip them to reach the world with the gospel. Thanks to Simon Baker, Emily Shore and Dev Lunsford for your work on proofing, editing, typesetting and designing the book: you guys are the best.

Thanks to my Advance brothers who constantly inspire, challenge and encourage me. What a privilege to spend time with you all, learn from you, and rejoice together over what God is doing.

To any and all with whom I have had the pleasure of discussing the contents of this book, and those who have listened to me preach on the subjects covered here: you have all shaped the content in some way, and

I am grateful for your listening ear, and any feedback that you offered along the way.

To my family, and particularly my parents, for pointing me to Christ throughout my life and revealing the gospel to me in word and deed. Thanks also to my dad for reading the manuscript of this book and helping to make it what it is; as ever, your insight, feedback and 'heresy checking' was so helpful.

I would like to dedicate this book to all those who make the focus of their life the preaching of the gospel in the power of the Spirit, and not least my brother in Christ and hero of the faith Billy Graham, who got the attention of God in a way that I hope many more will, for the glory of the kingdom. Oh, what a celebration he must have come home to! Thank you Jesus.

NOTES

1. Thomas B. Kilpatrick, *New Testament Evangelism,* (Hodder: London, 1901), 19.

2. As for what a Brit and an Italian Neo-fascist were doing having a late night conversation about Jesus in the middle of a street in Brooklyn, I will leave that to your imagination; it will likely be more interesting than the reality.

3. We are saved by faith alone, as Paul asserts repeatedly, but in James 2:14-18 the author presents deeds as the authentication of a claim to faith. In other words, if the Bible teaches that becoming a new creation is the hope of the gospel, both in the future perfection of heaven and also in the here and now, then the evidence of a person's salvation should be visible, not just in the claims of their mouth but in the actions of their life (an evidence of transformation). In his excellent, timely and recommended book, *Whatever Happened To The Gospel,* RT Kendall argues strongly that this way of thinking will always lead to us assuming that works will save us. I think he overstates his case a little, and personally hold that whilst we are saved by faith alone,

true faith in Jesus Christ will be evidenced by the kind of lives we live. The deeds do not save us, they are simply the external evidence of the internal submission to Christ's Lordship. On this point I agree with RT that our deeds are best understood as actions to reveal gospel identity to the world, rather than to assure us of our own salvation. Ultimately, God knows what is in our hearts despite outward appearances, both positive and negative.

4. This is excepting, of course, the element of adult life that involves impressing young people with my FIFA skills, or at least beating them 8-0 to teach them an important lesson in humility.

5. I don't believe you can simply state John 3:16 and pat yourself on the back for sharing the gospel. Indeed, the words of Jesus here are part of a longer conversation about the good news with Nicodemus, who doesn't seem to get it at first but needs further explanation and revelation.

6. 'I must preach that should someone hear me only once before he dies, he will have heard not just a part, but the entire way of salvation and in the proper way for it to take root in his heart.' A.H. Francke.

7. Tom Wright lays out a striking lament of this approach to gospel preaching in *Simply Good News* (SPCK: London, 2015), 4ff.

8. I sometimes hear it preached that, 'Even if you were the only person to have lived, Jesus would still have

died for you,' and while this is a powerful reflection on God's love for each individual, it can also be unhelpfully misleading. After all, this is not what actually happened: Jesus died for *all*, and now invites you to be part of the redemptive plan of salvation that you have already received. The gospel is not just for you, and not just about you; it is for all people, at all times and in all places, and is, first and foremost, about the glory of God himself.

9. John Wimber & Kevin Springer, *Power Evangelism* (Chosen Books: Grand Rapids, 2014) 28.

10. I should note that I personally believe the death cries of evangelistic freedom in the West are hugely exaggerated. In my experience, there are few areas in which genuine limitation has come into play, and there is a general openness within society to explore issues of faith and meaning as the world becomes increasingly unpredictable and insecure.

11. It's possible he didn't actually say this, or that he phrased it in a different way, but the sentiment holds up.

12. Michael Green, *The Empty Cross Of Jesus* (Hodder: London, 1984), 12.

13. If you want to get to grips with getting the most out of your Bible reading then I highly recommend *How To Read The Bible For All Its Worth* (Fee/Stewart, 2014, 4th ed.).

14. Ps. 14:1.

15. A problem not exclusive to the Bible. Other religious texts, literature, philosophy, political writings, and more, have all been used in ways the authors did not intend. We don't have space here to explore this fully but there are three basic ways to discern the truth of the written word:

    1. **The truth is in the interpretation** – This is obviously problematic, as truth becomes subjective and the same passage can mean different things to different people. This may be fine for ambiguous works such as poetry, but in truth claims such as, 'I am the way, the truth and the life…' a subjective view will not do. Absolute truth does not change based on your interpretation or your beliefs; it is either true or it is not. For example, God either exists, or he does not, irrespective of your belief.

    2. **The truth is in the text** – Also problematic, for what are we to do when the text is misprinted? If the truth is found exclusively in the text, any errors must be assumed as truth which can lead to complete nonsense! Not only that but the 'plain meaning' of any text is not equally plain to all, and so interpretation will still be challenging even when the text is 100% accurately presented.

    3. **The truth is in the author's intent** – Guess what, also problematic! But only because intent can be hard to establish. Despite this, it is clearly the best

way to discern truth: figuring out, to the best of our ability, what the author intended to communicate. In the case of the Bible, this is done through the reading of Scripture *in context* (that is: time and place of writing, intended audience, and context within Scripture, i.e. working outwards from verse to chapter, to book, to other writings from the same author, to testament [Old or New], to the whole of scripture). Christianity is the pursuit of truth, so we must all be committed to the task of understanding the Bible to the best of our (Spirit-empowered) ability.

16. Haddon Robinson, *Biblical Preaching,* (Baker Academic: Grand Rapids, 1980), 9.

17. 'Considerable care was taken to ensure that seekers really knew the gospel for themselves and to see that they were well grounded in the basic content and practices of the faith. This was a slow process, but it was absolutely essential if commitment was to be substantial and long-lasting.' William J. Abraham, 'A Theology of Evangelism: The Heart of the Matter' in Chilcote, Paul W., and Laceye C. Warner (eds.), *The Study of Evangelism: Exploring a Missional Practice of the Church,* (William B. Eerdmans Publishing Company: Grand Rapids, 2008).

18. That is the best anti-authority story I have: hiding a VHS tape from my chemistry teacher. Evidently, the

biker jacket/toothpick combo was always going to be a distant, anti-establishment pipe dream.

19. The kingdom of God is most basically understood as God's reign and rule. However, the Bible also uses this language to describe both a current realm where we can experience something of his blessings today, and a future realm where we will experience the fulness of his reign eternally. Both ideas are to be understood as God's kingdom.

20. 'The characteristic features of Jesus' [message] are… (1) the proclamation of the kingdom of God, both its imminence and its presence… (2) the call for repentance and faith in face of the end time power and claim of God… (3) the offer of forgiveness and a share in the messianic feast of the new age, with its ethical corollary of love.' James D.G. Dunn, *Unity and Diversity in the New Testament,* (SCM Press: London, 1977), 16.

21. For interesting discussion of Jesus' kingdom preaching, see William Brosend, *The Preaching of Jesus*, (Westminster John Knox Press: Louisville, 2010), 70ff.

22. N.T. Wright helpfully explains Jesus' message to his Jewish audience, while maintaining its relevance for us today, in *Jesus and the Victory of God,* (SPCK: London, 1996) and in a simplified and highly readable form in *Simply Good News*, (SPCK: London, 2015).

23. I am regularly asked the question, 'Can someone lose their salvation?'. I do not think you will ever

successfully and satisfyingly answer this question until you understand salvation in kingdom terms. I am tempted to explain further, but perhaps allowing you to connect these dots as you further study the gospel as kingdom reality will be a more fruitful teaching exercise.

24. Perhaps you can now connect the dots presented by the previous note.

25. William J. Abraham, 'A Theology of Evangelism: The Heart of the Matter' in Chilcote, Paul W., and Laceye C. Warner (eds.), *The Study of Evangelism: Exploring a Missional Practice of the Church,* (Eerdmans: Grand Rapids, 2008), 24.

26. If you can watch the end of E.T. without crying you are beyond my help!

27. At the risk of sounding like a baby-hating maniac, I just don't generally find babies to be particularly cute. I've learned over the years that this line of thinking is more offensive to people than pretty much anything else I could confess, but now you know. And I sense that you are quietly judging me as you read this.

28. Frank Turek, *Stealing From God,* (NavPress: Colorado Springs, 2014), 216-217.

29. It is worth reflecting here that if apologetics can sometimes be guilty of relying too heavily on reason rather than the Spirit's power to bring hearts to life, overly emotive preaching can sometimes fall into the trap of being manipulative, once again putting too

much stock in *our* ability to win people for Christ, rather than allowing the Spirit to work through our simple proclamation. Food for thought on both ends of the spectrum.

30. We could also explore the role of signs and wonders in evangelism at this stage, but space is limited so I will keep the focus on preaching in the power of the Spirit.

31. Attempts to find a uniform message have proved somewhat divisive but there is much to recommend C.H. Dodd's exploration of the early church *kerygma* (gk: *proclamation*, but Dodd and others also use the term to mean the *content* of the gospel message) in *The Apostolic Preaching and its Developments* (1936), which lays out a six-point summary of the content of the apostolic preaching. Any good NT theology or dictionary will include a summary of the *kerygma*, along with some discussion of its strengths and weaknesses, champions and detractors.

32. '...the focus [in Acts] shifts from announcement of the dawning reality, which is not denied in any way, to the basis, the grounds or the agency that makes the new reality a possibility. *What the kingdom depends on has become the good news.*' Donald A. Hagner, *The New Testament: A Historical and Theological Introduction,* (Baker: Grand Rapids, 2012), 311-313. Hagner also offers three basic reasons as to why the disciples may have moved away from direct kingdom language in their preaching:

1. Talk of a kingdom other than the Roman Empire could be misunderstood as treasonous.
2. The concept of the kingdom had Jewish roots and would not be easily understood by Gentile audiences.
3. As the church began to understand what Jesus had done, a new language was able to be employed that focussed on the fruit of the kingdom in the present age – the effects of Christ.

33. James D.G. Dunn, *Unity and Diversity in the New Testament,* (SCM Press: London, 1977), 20-21.

34. '...we may with some confidence accept the sermons in Acts, not indeed as a transcript of what was said, nor even as a summary of the addresses... but as a reliable sample of the way in which the earliest Christians set about convincing the first Jews of Jerusalem... of the truth of the Christian proclamation.' Michael Green, *Evangelism in the Early Church,* (Hodder: London, 1970), 69.

35. Michael Wilcock, *The Message of Luke's Gospel,* The Bible Speaks Today (InterVarsity Press: Downers Grove, 1979), 27.

36. The resurrection is apparently awkward for many believers too, as it was recently reported that a staggering 23% of British 'Christians' (from a survey of 2,010 British adults) do not believe the resurrection was a real event! Cultural Christianity, rather than true relationship, is the pathway to this kind of conclusion.

Faith in Jesus Christ is rendered meaningless without the resurrection (1 Cor. 15:14). For survey results see, http://www.bbc.com/news/uk-england-39153121

37. Michael Green, *Evangelism in the Early Church,* (Hodder: London, 1970), 54-55.

38. For example, do a quick Google search for 'the Engel scale'.

39. Sadly, not for the first time in my life. It probably also didn't help that this occurred during a brief phase where I sported orange and pink hair, having tried to self-bleach it blonde and add red highlights, so I probably looked like an unhinged maniac even before I opened my mouth. In my defence, we had only just left the glory days of the 90s: it was a different time, a better time.

40. Oh, and I guess a third lesson is that evangelism is hard when you have orange and pink hair.

41. David Platt, *Counter Culture,* (Tyndale: Carol Stream, 2015), 1.

42. Many don't like the confrontational nature of street preachers who shout about Jesus outside Boots. Aside from sympathising that people should be allowed to buy their deodorant in peace and recognising that there are possibly more effective methods of sharing the good news, we must not lose sight of the fact that the message of the gospel *is* confrontational. It forces you to confront your sin and the devastating temporal and

eternal consequences of it, whilst revealing the glorious hope found in King Jesus.

43. Jesus' interaction with the two disciples on the road to Emmaus is a great example of questioning, listening, questioning and revelation, see Lk. 24:13-32.

44. Ted Turnau, *Popologetics: Popular Culture in Christian Perspective*, (P&R Publishing: Phillipsberg, 2012).

45. An interesting recent example of this was hugely popular grime artist Stormzy's track *Blinded By Your Grace, Pt.2*, the lyrics of which are as profoundly worshipful to God as any contemporary worship song. And yet the rest of the songs on his album feature misogyny, endorsements of violence and drug culture, sexual material and strong language. Affirming the lyrics of one song does not mean affirming his entire body of work, nor does it mean affirming how he lives out his faith. But it can be a great conversation starter about why his lyrics are so powerful, and also why the expression of his faith in Jesus in the rest of his life could be problematic to the kind of living God is calling people to. In short, this hugely popular and widely accessible cultural touchstone offers us a great connection point.

46. Actually, Paul doesn't just use some cultural reference points here, he adapts his whole style of preaching to help this unique audience of Greek philosophers and scholars understand what he is saying, using classical rhetoric to deliver his message. Paul's *primary* concern

is the truth of the message, but he is also concerned that the message can be received and understood. Those who contend that Paul's method here saw limited success are frankly missing the point that he saw *any success at all* in an otherwise exclusively pagan environment.

47. Paul Copan & Kenneth Litwak, *The Gospel in the Marketplace of Ideas*, (IVP: Nottingham, 2014), 131.

48. To be fair, the last time I preached at a seniors group at least half the room fell asleep, so a bit of Calvin Harris might have been helpful. I could've used it as a wake-up siren every five minutes.

49. 'Many of the Samaritans from that town believed in him because of the woman's testimony, "He told me everything I've ever done."' (Jn. 4:39, NIV)

50. 'People need time and relationship to process another worldview. We can be those who, through friendship and conversation, put a pebble in the spiritual shoes of our secular-minded friends to help them recognise inconsistencies in their philosophy of life and become uncomfortable with that way of thinking and then consider the Christian faith to be a viable alternative.' Copan & Litwak, *The Gospel in the Marketplace*, 153.

51. I begged my dad to take me back in to see the film again but I don't have a memory of him doing that. I suspect he tried to occupy me with something else until I forgot about it, and yet here we are, decades later, with it still burned into my memory.

52. See Green, H., Mcginnity, A., Meltzer, Ford, T., Goodman, R. 2005 Mental Health of Children and Young People in Great Britain: 2004. Office for National Statistics. And, http://visual.ons.gov.uk/what-are-the-top-causes-of-death-by-age-and-gender/.

53. Jerry M. Henry, 'Trinity,' ed. Chad Brand et al., *Holman Illustrated Bible Dictionary* (Holman Bible Publishers: Nashville, 2003), 1625.

54. Occasionally, however, it refers to the patriarchs (Ps. 105:15), to a prophet (1 Kings 19:15), to the Servant of the Lord (Isa. 61:1), or to the cherub appointed for the protection of Israel (Ezk. 28:14).' O. A. Piper, 'Messiah,' ed. Geoffrey W Bromiley, The International Standard Bible Encyclopedia, Revised (Eerdmans: Grand Rapids, 1979–1988), 330.

55. 'the idea of the true god being king was tied in with the dream of holy revolution. 'No king but God!' was the slogan that fired the revolutionaries. It gave them courage to do the unthinkable: to tear down the eagle from outside the Temple.' N.T. Wright, *Jesus and the Victory of God*, (SPCK: London, 1996) 203-204.

56. 'In the case of the anointing of kings and prophets, however, the symbolism of the physical act seems to have gone beyond simply setting the person apart from others. In such cases the anointing also served to convey power and ability to perform the function for which one was being anointed. It further designated that the person had been chosen by God (1 Sam. 9:16),

and so kings in particular could be referred to as 'the Lord's anointed' (24:6). Timothy B. Cargal, 'Anoint,' ed. David Noel Freedman, Allen C. Myers, and Astrid B. Beck, *Eerdmans Dictionary of the Bible* (Eerdmans: Grand Rapids, 2000), 66.

57. Morris, *Matthew*, 421.

58. Not, generically, *a human.*

59. For a more detailed look at Jesus' claims of divine identity, see John Stott, *Basic Christianity*, New edition (InterVarsity Press: Nottingham, 2008), 31ff.

60. Piper, *Messiah*, 335.

61. 'Perhaps nothing shows the centrality of a messianic mentality more than the name by which Jesus came to be referred, Jesus Christ. Jesus' messianic position had become so attached to him that it was the best way to refer to him.' Vanhoozer, *Dictionary for Theological Interpretation*, 505. And we haven't even discussed the meaning of the name Jesus itself – 'Yahweh Will Save'. It's almost as if the Bible is trying to tell us something.

62. As it was too much for the rich young man that Jesus spoke with in Matthew 19:16-30.

63. 'At the cross God in Christ became our substitute to bear the punishment for our sins... The God-man propitiated our sin. This fact, that God the Judge, the 'Lord of glory' himself (1 Cor. 2:8), accepted the punishment due us, suggests that the penalty for sin against the Infinite is infinite. Questions will remain. But believers personally know God's love in Jesus

Christ. And their response to a lost world will parallel that of their Lord, who humbled himself to our condition, suffered, and died for the wicked.' Timothy R. Phillips, 'Hell,' *Evangelical Dictionary of Biblical Theology*, Baker Reference Library (Baker Book House: Grand Rapids, 1996), 340.

64. 'final punishment is pictured as outer darkness (Mt. 8:12; 22:13; 25:30). This suggests that both fire and darkness are metaphors used to represent the indescribable. 'I never knew you; depart from me, you evildoers' (Mt. 7:23); 'Truly, I say to you, I do not know you' (Mt. 25:12). Exclusion from the presence of God and the enjoyment of his blessings—this is the essence of hell.' George Eldon Ladd, *A Theology of the New Testament*, ed. Donald A. Hagner, Rev. ed. (Eerdmans: Grand Rapids, 1993), 196.

65. The picture the Bible paints of heaven tells us that in this perfect eternity, 'Believers will be like Christ (Rom. 8:29; 1 Cor. 15:49; Phil. 3:21; 1 John 3:2) and be with him (John 14:3; 2 Cor. 5:8; Phil. 1:23; Col. 3:4; 1 Thess. 4:17), sharing his glory (Rom. 8:18, 30; 2 Cor. 3:18; 4:17; Col. 3:4; Heb. 2:10; 1 Pet. 5:1) and his reign (2 Tim. 2:12; Rev. 2:26–27; 3:21; 20:4, 6). As children of God they will enjoy perfect fellowship with him (Rev. 21:3, 7), worshipping him (7:15; 22:3) before his face (Matt. 5:8; 1 Cor. 13:12; Rev. 22:4). Scripture portrays believers in a restored paradise (Luke 23:43; Rev. 2:7; 22:1–5) and the new Jerusalem (Heb.

12:22; Rev. 21). God's people share table fellowship at an eschatological banquet (Matt. 8:11; Mark 14:25; Luke 14:15–24; 22:30) or wedding feast (Matt. 25:10; Rev. 19:9)' Kevin J. Vanhoozer et al., eds., *Dictionary for Theological Interpretation of the Bible* (SPCK/Baker Academic: London/Grand Rapids, 2005), 440.

66. John R. W. Stott, *The Cross of Christ* (Downers Grove, IL: IVP Books, 2006), 63.

67. Andrew H. Trotter Jr., "Cross, Crucifixion," *Evangelical Dictionary of Biblical Theology*, Baker Reference Library (Grand Rapids: Baker Book House, 1996), 137.

68. Stott, *The Cross of Christ*, 171–173.

69. 'The Gospel of Jesus Christ: An Evangelical Celebration' is copyright ©1999 by the Committee on Evangelical Unity in the Gospel, P. O. Box 5551, Glendale Heights, IL 60139–5551.

70. 'When I Survey The Wondrous Cross', Isaac Watts.